IRISH ROGUES, RASCALS AND
SCOUNDRELS

X

DISCARD

IRISH ROGUES, RASCALS AND SCOUNDRELS

Padraic O'Farrell

THE MERCIER PRESS

The Mercier Press
PO Box 5, 5 French Church Street, Cork
24 Lower Abbey Street, Dublin

ISBN 1 85635 006 1

DA
916
.O42
1992
cop.1

For many good friends who have been victims of real rogues and scoundrels.

Printed in Ireland by Colour Books Ltd.

CONTENTS

ACKNOWLEDGMENTS

I wish to thank the Tessa Swayle Agency for permission to quote from Brendan Behan's *The Quare Fellow*, Seamus de Burca for permission to quote from *The End of Mrs Oblong* and Jean Binnie for her assistance with my research into James Barry. The following also gave considerable assistance: The National Library and its staff; Westmeath County Library, especially Tony Cox and Carmel Geraghty; Tim Cadogan, Cork County Library; Vincent Kelly, *Cork Examiner*; Hugh Leonard; Pádraig Folen; John Condon; Col Jim Croke; Frank Columb and John Finegan. Seamas Ó Cualain, An Spidéal and Gerry Naughton, Galway gave generously of their time and hospitality and as always, my wife Maureen and family gave full support.

INTRODUCTION

A rogue is a dishonest or unprincipled person but in a jocular context it is a mischievous child, a waggish individual or an inferior, perhaps defective, specimen among many that are acceptable. These are dictionary definitions but dictionaries can never define the Irish rogue. This character may well be dishonest or unprincipled. More often he is a 'likable rogue' – a rascal and a scoundrel tolerated for his fun and his penchant for taking the harm out of his indiscretions by some redeeming act. Irish facetiousness towards the species may be judged by the parental chastisement that is nearer an endearment: 'You're a right little rascal'.

A book of Irish rogues, therefore, must contain an assortment of roguish characters, a cross-section of this diverse breed. Mine is a personal selection, chosen after careful consideration, for many would be entitled to dishonourable mention. If the reader or his favourite rogue are not included, may I hide behind the Irish saying: 'I do not know if he is fool or a rogue'.

Padraic O' Farrell

1

THE SHAM SQUIRE

Mr Francis Higgins, 72 St Stephen's Green, Dublin was a shoe-black and later the proprietor of a basement huckster shop close to Green Street courthouse. A slight casual encounter with the Earl of Clonmel, John Scott, was developed and used by the ambitious Higgins to advance himself. Scott was Chief Justice of the King's bench, who as Attorney-General had been dismissed for claiming that England had no authority to bind Ireland by Acts of Parliament. Higgins had no such noble inclinations, however, because he was heavily involved in the betrayal of Lord Edward Fitzgerald, the United Irishman.

His parents, Patrick and Mary were humble people from Downpatrick, Co. Down. They moved to Dublin where Francis was born in a cellar and reared as a Catholic. His father became an attorney's clerk and Francis earned some money tending to the needs of patrons of Fishamble Street music-hall by ferrying porter in pewter tankards from a nearby inn. Red-headed and humped, the lad also swept paths outside shops. After a spell shoe-shining and huckstering, he became an attorney's clerk for the firm of Bourne, St Patrick's Close. There he forged documents purporting to establish him as a man of property, related to Lord Clonmel. He became a Protestant too, and all to impress a lady of means. Indeed, there are several accounts of Higgins changing his religion one way or another, in order to benefit financially. Also, there are charges of his befriending servants of judges, riding in their carriages and the like in order to compound his image. Around 1766 a grand jury found against Higgins. In its bill he is described as:

> a person of evil name, fame, and dishonest conversation, and a common deceiver and cheat, not minding to gain his livelihood by truth and honest labour, but devising to cheat, cozen and defraud William Archer of his moneys, fortune, and substance, for support of the profligate life of him, the said Francis Higgins, and with intent to obtain Mary Anne Archer in marriage, and to aggrieve, impoverish and ruin her, and with intent to impoverish the said William Archer, his wife, and all his family, by wicked, false and deceitful pretences. The said F. Higgins, by the same wicked pretences, procured Mary Anne Archer to be given in marriage to him, to the great damage of the said William Archer, to the great discomfort, prejudice, injury, and disquiet of mind of the said Mary Anne and the rest of the family, to the evil example of all others and against the peace of our said Lord the King, his crown and dignity.[1]

Evidence told how the couple married and moved to Lucan. Mary Anne found Higgins undesirable and ran home. Higgins chased her and caught up on her as she entered her own house. There was a violent struggle with her mother who tried to prevent him from entering. Mrs Archer was injured. Higgins was imprisoned in Cutpurse Row but when the case was heard and he was found guilty, he got off with a year in jail and a nickname, for Judge Robinson referred to him as a 'Sham Squire'.

Mary Anne gave birth but gave the infant into the care of a friend with the warning that Higgins was never to know its whereabouts. When she died of a broken heart, Higgins tried to discover the whereabouts of his offspring but failed. He married a female worker in the prison (whose father had been Daniel O'Connell's gaoler), proving again that in spite of a hump and gross appearance, this strange mixture of coarseness and humanity had a way with the ladies. After his release he became a hosier at The Wholesale and Retail Connemara Sock and Stocking Warehouse, Smock Alley. He was President of the Guild of Hosiers in 1775. Ambitious in the extreme, Higgins used every deceit possible to gain access to the Dublin social circle. The Lord Clonmel connection again helped when, around 1781, he became an attorney-at-law, with an address at Ross Lane. Most of his cases were at the court presided over by Scott.

Lord Carhampton, Governor and *Custos Rotulorum* of Dublin, patronised Higgins and appointed him a justice. As Colonel Luttrel, the British Cabinet had attempted to have Carhampton installed as representative for Middlesex, although he had lost an election there by 847 votes. He was later banished to Ireland where he directed large-scale half-hangings, pitch-cappings, cottage-burnings, rape, pillage and public floggings. He ill-treated a young whore in a house run by a Mrs Llewellyn. The madam was tried for complicity and sentenced to death. Francis Higgins, it was said, influenced the verdict being quashed. Dublin's humorists were quickly on target as they penned a parody on the popular 'The Night before Larry was Stretched', satirising an accomplice of Llewellyn's who was also on trial:

Oh the night ere Edgeworth was tried
The council all met in despair
The pressmen were there, and besides
A good doctor, a lord and a mayor.
Justice Sham then, a silence proclaimed
The bullies, they all of them harkened
Poor Edgeworth, sez he, will be framed,
His daylights might even be darkened
Unless we can lend him a hand.

11

The power of the press was apparent to Higgins so he lent money to the proprietor of the influential newspaper, the *Freeman's Journal*, but right away took steps to indict him for non-payment of the debt. Incredibly, he appears to have acquired ownership of the publication for quarter of its value on foot of this ploy.

Now the Sham Squire really swaggered before the lowly and crawled to the wealthy to whose company he had gained access. He wore a three-cocked hat, fringed with the down of a swan, bright yellow vest and breeches, a green, swallow-tailed jacket, violet gloves and tasselled boots. He carried a long, gold-knobbed staff. His indoor wear was augmented by diamond brooches and rings. For patronising the wealthy in his newspaper he received numerous favours. For a while he acted as coroner for Dublin city and as county sheriff. In the latter capacity, he tried certain obscure cases but acted with all the haughty grandeur of a high-court judge. For his ill-treatment of Catholic defendants and for his corrupt practices which made him rich, he gained a new nickname: Signor Shamando.

When the Marquis of Buckingham assumed the vice-regality of Ireland, it was feared that there would be no crowd to greet his arrival because of his unpopularity during a previous term in Ireland as Lord Temple. Francis Higgins saw an opportunity to curry favour. He hired a mob, fitted them with silken ropes and harness and had them drag the dignitary's carriage to Dublin Castle. Continuing his attempts to please the establishment, Higgins changed the thrust of the *Freeman's Journal* to being a staunch supporter of the government. Shamando moved to a fashionable Huguenot house at 72 St Stephen's Green. He dined with judges and revelled with the leading socialites of Dublin. He also became involved in the running of a secret gambling-house of low repute in

Crane Lane, a stone's throw from Dublin Castle and the office of the Board of Police. Dublin balladeers noticed and Higgins found himself in their song-sheets:

> *Alas! All gone! may every virtue weep,*
> *Shamando lives and Justice lies asleep.*
> *How shall I wake her? Will not all the cries*
> *Of midnight revels, that ascend the skies,*
> *The sounding of dice-box, and the shrieking whore*
> *The groans of all the destituted poor*
> *Undone and plundered by this outcast man,*
> *Will not these wake her?*

At this stage Higgins was overweight and pockmarked, a disgusting sight. He was lampooned in cartoons but among his friends he was welcomed at table for his humour. He had a country seat at Kilmacud where he was pleasured by women procured for him through a flashman. Instead of paying them, however, he forced them to pay him, under threat of dragging them to his court, charged with prostitution. In his gambling-house he employed men to cheat patrons and to foment troubles, then recommend their master as solicitor to the wrongdoers. The *Dublin Evening Post* described it as:

> a notorious school of nocturnal study in the doctrine of chances; a school which affords to men of the town an ample source of ways and means in the pluckings of those unfledged green-horns who can be inveigled into the trap; which furnishes to the deluded apprentice a ready mart for the acquisition of experience, and the disposal of any loose cash that can be purloined from his master's till; which affords to the working artisan a weekly asylum for the reception of that stipend which honest industry should allot to the purchase of food for a wife and children; and which affords to the spendthrift shopkeeper a ready transfer office to make over the property of his creditors to the plunder of knaves and sharpers.[2]

John Magee, editor of the *Dublin Evening Post* was relentless in his criticism of Higgins. Often, he included Lord Chief Justice Clonmel (John Scott) in his diatribe so Higgins drew Clonmel's attention to this and they connived to have Magee charged. Clonmel sought surety of £7,800 (an enormous figure at the time) on each of four charges brought by Higgins and others, including Richard Daly of Crowe Street Theatre, a duellist who had also killed a marker with a billiard-ball. Lord Clonmel heard the cases himself. An amusing anecdote tells how Magee, during the hearing, referred to Higgins as The Sham Squire. Lord Clonmel rebuked him, saying he would not allow any nicknames in his court. Magee retorted, 'Very well, John Scott!' When Magee was acquitted, the conspirators sought unsuccessfully to have him certified insane.

Now Higgins had his own elegant coach, with yellow trim and coat of arms tastefully emblazoned on its brown panels. He scoffed at denouncement from the pulpit, in spite of which he attended regularly at St Audeon's church. Sometimes he even dispensed charity as he drove away. He presided at Kilmainham court with John Toler (who would become Lord Norbury) but also occupied the Lord Mayor's bench on occasions. The wealth from his extortion, his gambling-house and his newspaper was further enhanced by gratuities from government, earned by informing.

On the bridge over the Liffey at Leixlip at twilight on a day in 1798, a young yeoman sentinel questioned a peasant. The stranger wore a frieze coat and corduroy knee-breeches and drove a few sheep. Sentinel Nicholas Dempsey waved on the disguised Lord Edward Fitzgerald, leader of the military organisation of the United Irishmen who supported revolution without waiting for French assistance. He went into hiding in Dublin and continued with his preparations for insurrection. From one house to another he moved to avoid capture. On 15 May 1798, Dublin Castle issued the following Proclamation:

> The Lord Lieutenant and Privy Council of Ireland have issued a proclamation declaring that they have received information upon oath, that Lord Edward Fitzgerald has been guilty of High Treason, and offer a reward of £1,000 sterling, to any person who shall discover, apprehend, or commit him to prison.[3]

On 17 May Major Sirr was notified of Fitzgerald's whereabouts by the under-secretary. Three days later, an account of Fitzgerald's capture was published by the Castle. It described how the house of a feather-merchant in Thomas Street was raided by the notorious Major Sirr and his men and how Fitzgerald was wounded, captured and sent to Newgate prison having put up a spirited resistance. He died there on 4 June from his wounds.

Many years afterwards, a second-hand book-dealer in Henry Street bought some discarded documents and publications from an official of Dublin Castle. A record of secret service monies expended during 1798 revealed the entry: 'June 20th, F.H. Discovery of L.E.F., £1,000.'[4] Irishmen argued the probability of its alluding to Higgins. Others had been suspected of informing and Higgins certainly did not convey the information direct. But the Sham Squire was certainly not beyond getting somebody else to do the talking while he collected the reward. It became one of the great talking-points of the period. Everyone knew that Higgins plied information to keep the establishment on his side. But was he guilty in this instance?

The correspondence of Lord Cornwallis, Lord Lieutenant and Commander-in-Chief eventually threw some light on the case. First of all it revealed that Cornwallis received notification from the under-secretary that Higgins, among others, was entitled to share the secret-service allotment of £1,500 per annum. But the most damning and aggravating entry recommended Higgins for a pension of £300. The proprietor of the *Freeman's Journal*, said the under-secretary, 'was the person who procured for me all the intelligence respecting Lord Edward Fitzgerald, and got — to set him, and has given me much information'.[5] The part played by Francis Higgins was made clear but the mystery of the unnamed individual who did the setting still caused controversy. It was generally accepted that an associate of Higgins' called Magan was the man in question. He had helped the Sham Squire to organise the reception for Lord Buckingham and remained a drinking and dining partner of his.

A person's last will and testament often reveals characteristics that were not apparent during life. Higgins was no exception. He left £1,000 to a female friend, £100 to his housekeeper, £50 to an asylum for ruined merchants, £100 to the Lying-In Hospital provided a bed was named in his honour. He left £20 to the Blue Coat Hospital, £400 to a Colonel O'Kelly, £100 to Fr O'Leary and many smaller bequests. The Sham Squire wanted no sham tomb; it was to be a slab, well secured with brick-work, stone and lime, in Kilbarrack cemetery.

Francis Higgins died on 19 January 1802. Dublin people would say, thirty-seven years later, that the 'Big Wind' was as bad as the night the Sham Squire died. His Kilbarrack tomb was fashioned in 1804. A list of his larger bequests was carved upon it; also the epitaph 'Sacred to the Memory of Francis Higgins.' It did not always receive the respect due to a grave; one of Dublin's aldermen it was said, never passed the graveyard without dismounting from his horse, going to the tomb and screaming insults at the Sham Squire. Another 'old gentleman of eccentric disposition, who lived at Howth, was in the habit, on his way to Dublin, of halting at Kilbarrack and dancing Jig Polthogue on the flat tombstone'.[6] Watty Cox implied that Higgins realised that 'religion was a good disposable article in skilful hands'; he was comparing a protégé called Conway who, he claimed called to the Squire's tomb 'and after reading with impassioned energy the eulogium it bore, burst into tears, and declared upon his honour, the composition was unequalled in the history of sepulchral literature'.[7] Later on, a sledge-hammer was used to smash part of the imposing slab and although a reward was offered for information on the perpetrators, none was forthcoming. Even when his escapades were almost forgotten, a roughly-hewn inscription appeared, defacing the complimentary inscription. Below a diagram of a gallows and a pike were the words:

Here lies the monster
Higgins,
Lord Edward Fitzgerald's informer.

2

A MEDICAL WONDER

Although women have served as soldiers in national armies for some time now, certain countries, including our own, stipulated that they should not be employed in operational units. In the middle of the last century, however, the thought of a woman serving in barracks, let alone on the battlefield, was unthinkable, especially in the ranks of the British army. Yet an Irish girl did just that. What is more, she adopted the guise of a man, challenged a number of colleagues to duels and fought at least one, then went on to become a top-ranking senior officer. She was known throughout her career as James Barry.

The English author and humorist, Edward Lear (1812–88) is credited with a line-drawing of Dr Barry, allegedly sketched in Corfu, when the lady was stationed there. It shows a rather old, uniformed officer, stooped and carrying a crop. Underneath is the legend: *Dr Barry (?) Insp Gen of Hosp.* Presumably because Her Majesty's army was embarrassed by Barry's escapade, it received little publicity other than a news' item in the Manchester *Guardian* after the surgeon's death.

There were two notable James Barrys in Cork in the eighteenth and nineteenth centuries. One (1741–1806) was an artist, described by contemporaries as a 'little, shabby, pockmarked man in a dirty old coat with a scarecrow wig, living for the most part on bread and apples.'[1] He moved to Dublin at the age of twenty-two. He was ever concerned about calumny and slander and felt that his artistic associates subjected him to both. Edmund Burke (1729–1797) supported him but was slighted as a result of Barry's persecution complex. The artist's work was considerable. An oil painting 'Iachimo and Imogen from Cymbeline' in The National Gallery of Ireland reminds us that Iachimo secretly studied details of the girl while she slept. This might lead to speculation on some reports of the lady surgeon being James' daughter. I will suggest otherwise, however.

The artist was born in Water Lane, Blackpool and became in turn a mason, a Henry Street innkeeper and a professor of painting at the Royal Academy of Arts. A Protestant, his Catholic wife reared the children in her own religion. James Barry had three brothers and a sister, Mary Anne. The brothers fell on hard times. After their mother's death, Mary Anne – a tough, greedy woman – deprived them of inheritance and turned a deaf ear to their subsequent pleas for financial assistance. She married Jeremiah Bulkley, a former weigh-bridge attendant who was sacked because of his religion and who turned instead to the family's grocery business. A daughter, Margaret, was born in 1789. Mary Anne attempted to get her father's house from James for Margaret, claiming that her husband and son had thrown her out. There is evidence, however, that she and Jeremiah promoted the career of a son, John, to such an extent that they themselves became penniless and Jeremiah was imprisoned for debts. John was a solicitor's apprentice in Dublin where he met a society lady called Ward. Her brother, General Ward had been put to the guillotine by Maximilian Robespierre, the French revolutionary, and the Bulkleys bought John a farm because the Wards wanted a man of property as a suitor. A move to England took place towards the end of 1804, and Mary Anne wrote to her artist brother from London on 14 January 1805:

What did you give my child when she was here last June, did you Ask her to Dinner, in short did you act as an Uncle or as Christian to a poor unprovided for Girl who had not been brought up to think of Labor and, Alas! whose Education is not finished to put her in a way to get Decent Bread for herself & whose share has been given to a Brother.[2]

When the artist died on 22 February 1806, Mary Anne pursued his substantial properties with vigour, becoming expert at dealing with Christie's, the Royal Academy of Arts, lawyers and financiers.

On 2 September 1808, John again wrote to his mother complaining about being unhappy and asking her to do something to promote him. He was a Royal York Ranger on board the *HMS Adriatic Transport* docked at Spithead, and was bound for the West Indies. An undated letter to him from Margaret may have been sent in reply. Purged of its archaic usages and misspellings it reads:

By this time I dare say you have experienced the wisdom or folly resulting from your substituting a musket for a goose-quill – either (in the opinion of a girl) may reflect honour on a man if used with spirit, in a good cause. Indeed, my dear John, a soldier fighting for his King and country and his rights as a Britisher or Hibernian in my mind acts nobly, honourably and gloriously, and the old phrase 'there is a reward in Heaven for all who die fighting for their country' is an article in my Creed and I most firmly believe in it. If you have not quite forgotten your Latin read what Horace says on the subject: *Dulce et decorum est pro patria mori*.[3] Was I not a girl I would be a soldier! However, I must honestly confess I would prefer a sword to a musket and I should like a pair of Colours at least; then I should use them to promote myself and perhaps you may also prefer these necessary appendages to a soldier. We must see what can be done for you. Write, therefore, an account of your situation and the names of some of the principal officers. John, write like a gentleman or Margaret will blush for you.[4]

The letter provides a hint of what was to come. In spite of Uncle James' estate, mother and daughter, then living at Charles Street, Hampstead Road, became hard-up and another letter suggests that Margaret was seeking employment with a lady in Camden town. At about twenty years of age, Margaret matriculated and in December 1809, enrolled at Edinburgh University, using her artist uncle's name, James Barry. She gave a younger age, perhaps to assist her disguise.

So Cork's second distinguished James Barry took the stage. Released from the debtor's jail, her father tried to contact her, without success. Margaret Bulkley had disappeared; James Barry (female) replaced her. On 14 December 1809, she wrote to her solicitor saying she was James Barry's nephew but calling Mary Anne Bulkley her aunt. Over a year later, she wrote to the controversial Venezuelan, General Francisco de Miranda who was in London trying to interest the British government in his recently developed plans for a new Inca empire. She begged discretion, referring to people not knowing anything about 'Mrs Bulkley's Daughter'.[5] Samples of Margaret Bulkley's and James Barry's writing bear credible similarities. Miranda's library at 27 Grafton Street was, at the time, one of the best private collections in London. 'It was indeed a very great privilege to be allowed to work [there] .... It was valued at £9,000, and estimated to contain about 6,000 volumes, on all subjects and in many languages, and – not least from young Barry's point of view – there was a collection of "treatises such as might be considered to form a tolerably complete Medical Library for a private gentleman".'[6]

Mary Anne Bulkley stayed with her daughter during her studies in Edinburgh, so she was in on the masquerade, obviously. She continued to press her solicitor for monies, some to pay Dr Barry's landlord, and for possession of the artist brother's house in Cork. To 301, South-wark High Street, London, mother and daughter returned in May 1812. James Barry had graduated and was study-ing surgery at Guy's Hospital and St Thomas'. She had planned to join General de Miranda, by then in command of the Venezuelan army and failing dictator. By the time she became a qualified surgeon, he had been captured by the Spanish authorities, shipped to Cadiz and imprison-ed. So James Barry undertook a bolder scheme. In 1813, claiming to be under nineteen years of age, she joined the British army's medical corps, still posing as a man and using her uncle's name.

With flaming red hair and high cheekbones she was handsome in her officer's uniform. After an initial posting at Plymouth, she served in various locations throughout the empire, becoming assistant-surgeon and surgeon to various units. Demonstrating considerable prowess in her profession, she practised in the Cape Colony in 1816, and was promoted to the staff there around 1825. James Barry's surgical skills received acclaim; perhaps her deli-cate female hands were more deft than those of her male colleagues. She was admired particularly for making quick and decisive diagnoses about treatment. Before Napoleon's death on St Helena, news of Barry's prowess reached the island and arrangements were being made to have her treat the defeated emperor when he died. It must be remembered that in those days amputation and other major operations were often carried out under pri-mitive conditions, without the aid of anaesthetics. A re-former, she displayed sympathy for the oppressed black population who endured floggings, infanticide, incarcer-ation and lived in filth within their miserable hovels. Like all competent people, she suffered malicious gossip. It may have been true that she became the lover of the gov-ernor, Lord Somerset; if so, she had nobody but herself to blame when the scandalmongers related a homosexual relationship! They went as far as nailing up a poster near the doctor's house which inferred a liaison between the couple. Arrests were made but a court hearing failed to convict anyone. The governor, Barry and assorted merchants all offered handsome rewards for information about the perpetrators, to no avail.

Certainly, James Barry could influence the governor. When she arrived in the Cape, lepers roamed about half naked and were shunned by society. Before she was a year there, the Heaven and Earth colony had been established in the Caledon district. Soon after she had got them rights to swim and to avail of facilities previously denied them. Their welfare was a burning issue with her always. Principled and dictatorial, she put up with no nonsense and her Irish temper made her the bane of many an incompetent junior's life. Yet she vehemently supported the rights of the under-privileged and volunteered to act as medical officer at the appalling prison called 'The Tronk' with its filthy dungeons and emaciated convicts. Once, it was said, she defended a sailor at a court-martial so passionately that the judge-advocate, annoyed at being browbeaten, gave the unfortunate seaman a period in detention as punishment. James Barry rode horses, drove a carriage and four, visited the theatre and went to fashionable balls. Her witty conversation made her popular at these. She wore a pea-green jacket, satin waistcoat and tight-fitting breeches called 'inexpressibles'. She made it her business to flirt with the ladies and even got the name of being a bit of a lady-killer! Yet there was some gossip about her femininity, about her ever so delicate touch, even about her being a woman – but the idea was so incredible that it was never given credence. James Barry fought a duel with pistols against the governor's aide-de-camp, Captain Cloete. Jealousy has been cited as the reason, for Cloete had suggested that the governor was having an affair with a Dutch lady guest. Neither party was injured in the duel. The only feminine trait on record is the ownership of a pet poodle which she called Psyche.

As assistant staff-surgeon in Mauritius, she so annoyed her superiors that she was sent home to England. Some reports suggest that her sex was discovered by a Mrs Fenton who rushed into her room without knocking and that Barry departed for England without official leave. In any event she was promoted Colonel of the 33rd Regiment of Foot in 1830.

During four years in Jamaica (1831–5) she proved her adroitness at spotting malingerers in a station that, with one in nine soldiers dying every year, had the second worst health record in the British empire. The scorching sun, the lack of tropical kit, the mosquitoes carrying their dreaded yellow fever, the disease-ridden marshes gave way to lashing rains, dampness and grime as the seasons changed. The same wooden troughs were used as urinals and wash-up sinks. Rum was the soldier's only comfort; if the army had welfare officers they were shirking their duty. They got drunk, received floggings for misconduct, then got drunk again.

Living amid death and depravity, Barry sent report after report to her overlords who lived a high social life. Before she left Jamaica, she had the pleasure of seeing slavery banned. Also, she had employed a former slave as a servant. She had become vegetarian and almost teetotal too.

After a short furlough in London, James Barry was posted to St Helena to supervise the civilian and military wards of its regimental hospitals. *En route*, there was an outbreak of smallpox on her ship. For quarantine reasons, her dog, Psyche, had to swim ashore at the Cape but the rest of her belongings were burnt. She completed the journey to St Helena in 1836 and occupied the Principal Medical Officer's home at Jamestown. Scurvy was rife and she campaigned to alter the troops' diet to combat dysentery. Venereal disease was common too, but Barry tended to ignore those suffering from it. Was this an early feminist gesture? Soldiers, sailors, men, women, maniacs and prostitutes were treated together in some wards. She contracted yellow fever at one stage. Court-martialled for misconduct, she conducted her own defence and was acquitted. There were other instances of disciplinary action against her, including demotion. In most cases they had to do with her breaking rules for the good of her patients. Eventually the governor of the island had her sent home under arrest. Six months later she was back in action – in the West Indies.

About the year 1840, Barry leap-frogged ranks and was promoted to Deputy Inspector General. That was in Corfu. Yet again she fell foul of the authorities because commonsense urged her to attempt to stop British soldiers being forced to drill in the midday heat. During a second visit there, she attempted to get posted to the front when the British entered the Crimean War. Thwarted, she then managed to get the war-wounded shipped to Corfu. But some reports suggest that she did get to the war-zone during a period of leave and that, furthermore, she had an altercation with the celebrated Florence Nightingale and kept the nurse standing in the blazing sun while she, on horseback, chided her. In mid-life, Barry was posted as Medical Inspector to Malta. She treated the dreaded cholera there. Her next posting was to Corfu, where she lived for some time. Canada was her final posting and its cold climate had an adverse effect on her health. Records of her sojourn there describe her as Inspector General. After forty-five years army service she retired on medical grounds in 1858 but it was not until her death on 15 July 1865 that her true sex was discovered. To guard her secret, she was hidden under copious nightclothes and blankets. She was then seventy-one years of age. No relative claimed the body. Some people speculated on her being the grand-daughter of a Scottish earl who loved and lived with an army medical officer throughout her service. A headstone at Kensal Green cemetery in London still preserved her secret. It read:

DR JAMES BARRY:
INSPECTOR GENERAL
OF ARMY HOSPITALS

DIED 15th JULY 1865
AGED 71 YEARS

The doctor's secret was revealed in the press a few days later. James Barry was, nonetheless, described as a superior type of person who had succeeded with a deception:

> so extraordinary that, were not the truth capable of being vouched for by official authority would certainly be deemed absolutely incredible. This gentleman had entered the army in 1813, had passed, of course, through the grades of assistant surgeon and surgeon in various regiments, and had served as such in various quarters of the globe. The motives that occasioned, and the time when commenced this singular deception are both shrouded in mystery. But thus it stands as an indisputable fact, that a woman was for 40 years an officer in the British service, and fought one duel and had sought as many more, had pursued a legitimate medical education, and received a regular diploma, and had acquired almost a celebrity for skill as a surgical operator.[7]

As the news spread, so did the stories, with a number of narrators telling how they suspected James of being a woman all along. A pair of liveried footmen were said to have called to Barry's Margate Street boarding house and removed Psyche, a ring and a mysterious black box. There was a tell-tale inscription on a ring! The box contained proof of her sex! – more and more did the outlandish tales proliferate. These reached a climax when one Sophia Bishop, an Irish charlady who had laid out Barry's corpse and witnessed the death certificate stated that the deceased Inspector General was a woman who had borne a child. The doctor who had signed the certificate of James Barry, male, was questioned. Yes, he said, the woman had told him she noticed that Barry was a woman and had pointed to what she considered were stretch-marks. His own conclusion, however, was that James Barry was a hermaphrodite.

Mary Anne Bulkley's daughter appears in the company of Irish rogues because evidence suggests that she pulled off the biggest confidence trick imaginable. At Marine Villa, Camps Bay, Cape Town, the ghost of Surgeon James Barry is said to walk with just the slightest trace of a feminine gait!

3

RENEGADE ARCHBISHOP

In Ireland, a religious turncoat is the most despicable of rogues so the rapacious Archbishop of Cashel, Miler Magrath has been held in contempt, particularly in Munster, for over three centuries. Near Ireland's penitential lake Lough Derg (St Patrick's Purgatory), in the teapot spout of Donegal that protrudes into Fermanagh, lay Termon Magrath. The existence of a monastery there was recorded as far back as 1290, when *The Annals of Ulster* noted that 'Gilla Adomhnain Magrath, Superior of Termon Dabheog died on October 20th of this year'. Folk history dates a priory of the Canons Regular of St Augustine on Lough Derg at 1134 and tells of Dervogilla, wife of Tiernan O'Rourke of Breffni, eloping with Dermot Mac-Murrough while her unfortunate husband was doing penance at St Patrick's Purgatory. Giraldus Cambrensis referred to the penitential island also.

During the Protestant Reformation, Henry VIII endowed loyal Irish chieftains with spoils and lands of monasteries. The Augustinian monastery in Termon Magrath was given to local chieftain, Donagh Magrath. During the reign of Elizabeth I, in 1596, the Calendar of the Patent Rolls 1596, Number 13, recorded a:

> surrender by Donagh Magrath chieftain of Termon Magrath and of his name in Ulster and Milerius Magrath, Archbishop of Cashell, his eldest son, to the Queen, of the lands and territory of Termon Magrath for the purpose of reducing the lands to English tenure and with the intent that they should be re-granted to Donough [sic] for life,

remainder to his eldest son Milerius for life.

Miler Magrath came from a branch of a family who were Bards of Thomond. Born about the year 1523, he was the eldest son of the minor chieftain who was Termoner or Erenach of the Lough Derg monastery. Miler joined the Franciscan order in 1540 and was ordained a Catholic priest nine years later. From 1556 to 1564, he ministered in the Netherlands and in Spain. Pope Pius V personally consecrated him on 12 August 1565 as Bishop of Down, the See founded by St Patrick. Queen Elizabeth, who denied the right of anyone but herself to confer episcopal status, seems to have turned a blind eye to this. On 31 May 1567 Magrath conformed and made his humble submission before Lord Deputy Sir Henry Sydney in Drogheda. This acknowledged the Queen's supremacy but she did not reciprocate with a Writ of Restitution confirming his appointment to Down. It has been argued that Magrath did not alter his doctrinal views but the fact that he apostatised is irrefutable, because he was appointed Protestant Archbishop of Clogher in 1570. He himself had asked for Down, with Cork and Cloyne his second preference. Clogher was a poor diocese. Its territories had been ravaged by wars and its revenues were meagre. The population was mainly Catholic, so Magrath's tithes amounted to very little. Within months, however, he was promoted to the archbishopric of Cashel and Emly. He assumed office on 3 February 1571.

Now Cashel's first Papal Archbishop after the Reformation was Fitzgibbon. He was appointed in 1567. A frequenter of the court of Philip II of Spain, he left there to take up his Cashel appointment. By the time he reached Tipperary, Elizabeth had installed Archbishop MacCaughwell, a Protestant, in Cashel. Fitzgibbon forced entry to the cathedral and took MacCaughwell prisoner and wounded him in an affray. Because of this assault, he had to return to Philip in 1569, where he attempted to prevail upon the King to meddle in Irish affairs for his benefit. Philip dismissed him with disdain.

Magrath, meanwhile, was appointed. Perhaps the new Pope, Pius V, hoped that Magrath would revert to Catholicism, for he did not replace Fitzgibbon. (The next mention of a Catholic Archbishop is O'Hurley's appointment by Pope Gregory XIII on 3 September 1581, three years after the exiled Fitzgibbon's death at sea). It is important to realise that in Elizabeth's reign Protestantism in Ireland was politicised and appointments to Sees were often of a perfunctory nature. The alleged apostasy might, therefore, have been disputed but for Magrath's marriage, in 1575, to Dame Amy O'Meara, daughter of John O'Meara of Lisanuisce, Co. Tipperary. This clearly contravened Roman Catholic rules on celibate clergy.

Clogher, meanwhile, was left the only Ulster dioceses without a reformation Bishop. Miler seized this chance to continue demanding for himself and his brother the benefits formerly exacted on the Pope's behalf. He even petitioned the Privy Council to formalise this arrangement until 'a man should be had by the state that would accept the Bishopric and observe Her Majesty's laws not only to diminish the Pope's authority but also to increase God's glory and Her Majesty's revenues.'[1] The Catholic Bishop of Clogher, Cornelius McArdle complained to the Lord Deputy.

On 14 May 1578 a Grant of English Liberty was made to Miler Magrath and his issue. The latter eventually comprised: Turlough, Redmond, Brian, Marcus, James, Mary, Cecilia, Anne and Elis [Alice?]. Turlough's line was to last into the seventeenth century; his first son, Sir John, was made a baronet by patent of 5 June 1629 and was County Sheriff for Tipperary in 1641. John's son, also Turlough, moved to Tulla, Co. Clare. Miler's second son, Redmond went to Clare too. The line survived in Kilbarron and a number of descendants served in the French army.

When Pope Gregory XIII finally deprived him of Down and Connor, in 1580, Magrath became a persistent beggar of favours, proclaiming poverty and hardship. Elizabeth seemed to hold him in some regard, for in 1582 he was commended and was granted the revenue of the temporalities and spiritualities of the See of Lismore and Waterford. In 1584 he petitioned for the surrender and re-grant of Termon Magrath and Termon Imogayne to his father, Donagh, with remainder to himself and further remainder to his sons. In the same petition he sought per-mission to hold fairs and markets in the towns of Carn and Cometh. When he went north to keep a watchful eye on his interests, he became a gambling, swashbuckling blade dressed in doublet of proof buff leather, jacket and breeches and carrying a sword. Accompanied by a retin-ue of servants he hunted the hills of Fermanagh and forced the clergy in the various deaneries to provide hos-pitality and defray his expenses.

After one of these forays, in October 1591, Bishop McArdle made a more spirited complaint to the Lord Deputy. Magrath, he claimed, had visited several times. During each period, he had twelve hounds and grey-hounds, each of which was cessed upon local clergy. They ate two quarts of meal, two of butter and two of milk each day. On the business side, Miler had commandeered £8 from a parson in Boherfellan as well as three dwelling-houses which he gave to his sister free of any rent to McArdle. In other areas he demanded and received amounts totalling £180, a considerable sum from a poor diocese. Eight brood mares, two horses and four cows were added to Miler's livestock too.

On 8 October 1597, he received the 'site, circuit and

precinct'[2] of the late priory and religious house of Thome, Co. Tipperary, as well as the properties and lands of Aughnameall, Envyne, Ballyboy, Aghincor and Killyertiragh. Perhaps Miler heard the story of the drunk staggering across the stepping stones and ejaculating: 'God is good but the devil isn't too bad either' because he still flirted with two religions. In July 1593, the Lord Deputy was forced to submit a formal complaint saying 'many Popish emissaries have nested in Ireland by the ArchBishop of Cashel's favour'.[3] In the same year he was accused of simony and extortion but the rogue went to London and submitted a written profession of his desire for the reformation of Ireland. The Lord Deputy's office announced the concern of the Queen and her officers for the state of religion, a worry not shared by Her Majesty's churchmen. Magrath, in particular, always had a poor mouth to make about his own poverty and evil case, the Lord Deputy declared. Magrath answered the charge stating:

> Where your Honour did write that I most irreligiously suffered the churches under me to lie like pig-stys [sic] and that I was not so bare left by the wars, but that I might remedy the same, I do confess the churches in the most parts and within five miles of Dublin itself to be like hogstys [sic], or rather, worse. Yet am I not in fault whereof, but rather the three sorts of people against whom I have no power, namely the traitors, The Papists and the soldiers.[4]

Magrath claimed that he had been beaten like a dog by a certain Captain Nuse within the precincts of his own broken and burned house at Lismore, Co Waterford. Sarcastically he added 'saving for credit's sake ... instead of a cudgel or a club, I was beaten and struck with pikes and halberds and shot at with bullets, which kind of credit I would rather lose than have'.[5]

Magrath's physical appearance was described about this time; he had a high forehead, an elongated visage with aquiline nose. He wore a goatee 'or square beard with imperial'. His countenance was shrewd, sullen and staid and he was attired in *calobium sendoris* (surplice).[6] Yet he survived in folk memory as an extremely handsome man.

When James I ascended the throne in 1603, the state of religion in the Kingdom of Ireland was still receiving adverse comment. Once again, Miler Magrath was singled out for particular mention among those who were described as being more fit 'to sacrifice the calf than to intermeddle with the religion of God'.[7] Another report on Magrath was submitted in 1608. He was housing his brother, two Jesuit priests and dispatching letters across the seas. He was accused of wasting funds and alienating the Lords of the manor-houses. Writing to the Earl of Salisbury in May 1606, Sir John Davys commented on the amount of demesnes in Magrath's care and on the deplorable state of prisons and public places. He claimed that there was but one churchgoer in Cashel 'for even the Archbishop's own sons, and sons-in-law, dwelling there, are obstinate recusants.'[8]

Miler Magrath still visited Clogher, keeping an eye on some property there and on Termon Magrath. He tried to have the See of Killala and Achonry annexed, claiming that he had lost Waterford and Lismore. (In 1582 and 1583, these were given to him pending an official appointment and his possession was renewed in 1592. He surrendered them in 1607). His life was one of avarice and double-dealing. He was not a credit to any religion and indeed he was paid little respect by either. Why Elizabeth I favoured him so much is a mystery. In his heyday he had the revenues of four Bishoprics and he appropriated the income from seventy livings and spread it among his own family. His daughter received the income from the parishes of Mortalstown and Ballydrinan, Lismore. Miler forced Rector O'Hogan of Fethard to share his income with Magrath's son, James. His fourth son, Marcus, administered another vicarage, although a layman and Miler's brother did likewise.

On 29 January 1612, the Apostolic Nuncio granted faculties to a certain Fr Mamin O'Doulery to receive Miler Magrath into the Catholic Church at his own request. Defenders say Miler kept this quiet in order to avoid a stigma of illegitimacy on his issue. As he approached the century in age, he erected a monument to himself in Cashel cathedral, opposite that of Edmund Butler. It was placed in a lofty position on the south side of the Choir, between the episcopal throne and the altar. A carved angel stood on each side. The head of the crucified Christ was depicted above, the pierced feet below. Mitred, with a pastoral staff in the hand, Miler's recumbent effigy seemed to detail Catholic vestments, as did its episcopal cross and rings on his hand raised in blessing. Behind it, a slab depicted St Patrick, similarly attired. The tomb was emblazoned with a coat of arms which resembled that of the Thomond bards, viz:

Argent, three lions passant gules.
Or, a dexter hand fesseways, couped at wrist ppr., holding a
cross formee fitchee azure.
Gules, a dexter hand fesseways, couped at wrist ppr., holding a
battleaxe or.
Argent, an antelope trippant sable attired or.

The epitaph, in Latin, could be translated so:

Patrick, the glory of our isle and gown,
First sat a Bishop in the See of Down.

> *Would that I, succeeding him in place*
> *As Bishop, had an equal share of grace.*
> *I served you, England, fifty years in jars,*
> *I pleased your princes in the midst of wars.*
> *Here where I'm laid, I'm not and so the case is*
> *I'm not in both, yet am in both the places. 1621.*
> *He that judgeth me is the Lord – Cor. 4*
> *Let him who stands take care lest he should fall.*

On 14 November 1612, Miler Magrath died, aged almost 100 years. There are those who say that he was never interred in his elaborate tomb. The enormity of the whole saga can be assessed when we discover that the reprobate's family were all reared in the Catholic religion and remained thus throughout their lives. His will bears testimony to this. Altered only to remove archaic forms of spelling and dating a summary reads:

Memorandum that on the 8th of November 1622 [sic], Miler Magrath, late Lord Archbishop of Cashel, at Cashel aforesaid, being sick of body, but of perfect memory and understanding, made his last will and nuncupative testament in manner and form following:

In the first place he bequeathed his soul to God, and wished his body to be buried in the cathedral church of Cashel.

Further, he left and bequeathed unto his son, Redmond Magrath, all such sums of money, arrears of rent and debts whatsoever due unto the said Miler, by bill, bond or any other manner of obligation, action or cause.

Also, he made, constituted and appointed the said Redmond Magrath his sole executor of that his last will and nuncupative testament.

Also, he wished all such pledges as lay upon his hands of the goods of any of his children formerly lent unto them, to be gratis restored unto his said children respectively, from whom the said pledges were for any such lended money received.

Also, he left and bequeathed all of his goods, real and personal, unto the said Redmond, to be divided by him in his discretion, between himself, the said Redmond, and the rest of the testator's children.

The aforesaid last will and nuncupative testament, the day, the year, and place aforesaid in manner and form before expressed, was made and declared by the said Miler before William James O'Dwyer, William Magrath and Rory Magrath.

Proved in the Prerogative Court, 16th day for the month of June 1624.[9]

Certain historians have defended Magrath, saying that he never disavowed his Catholic faith. During his fifty years reign as Archbishop of Cashel, however, he clearly exercised duplicity for his own gain. Not alone was he avaricious for himself, but he looked after the interests of his extended family, to the detriment of both Catholic and Protestant churches. This, when the actual number of Protestant souls under his care hardly amounted to a score. Such despicable behaviour makes the words 'rogue', 'rascal' or 'scoundrel' almost too gentle for Magrath.

4

HANDSHAKING POLITICIAN

Since Caesar was stabbed by his loyal henchman, politicians have been, often unfairly, regarded as 'thundering rogues' surrounded by 'handlers' who surpass their masters in wiles. Attendance at funerals, patting the baby on the head and other common touches have been added to by certain personalities with great success. Oliver Flanagan, the Laois–Offaly deputy, for instance, once canvassed upon a bicycle. He wore a type of sandwich-board with 'Here comes Oliver' on front and 'There he Goes' behind. It was remarkable to hear him rattling off the names of constituents and their specific house-numbers in some large town estate. But the man most remembered for political expediency (a skilled and refined form of roguery?) is Alfred Byrne TD, better known as Alfie, Lord Mayor of Dublin who was born in 1882.

Although some people claimed the Byrnes came from Wicklow, Alfie stoutly stated that his father, Thomas P. Byrne, was from Seville Place, in Dublin's dockland. Alfie created one of his many Irish bulls when he boasted of his father being from the parish of St Laurence O'Toole and 'all his life a member of the Amalgamated Society of Engineers'.[1] Trade Unionists started at a tender age in those days! A mercantile marine for fifty years, Thomas became unemployed when Alfie was thirteen years of age. The boy was forced to leave school and work a twelve hour day for two and sixpence a week selling theatre programmes in the streets. This was followed by a spell in the bicycle trade. He developed contacts with employees from the licensed trade and promoted agitation within their trade union.

By 1911, Alfie was known as 'The Boy Publican', being the proprietor of the 'Verdon Bar' as the Jim Larkin edited *Irish Worker* called his public house in Foley Street, close to Talbot Street. The paper told how he began life in:

> a 'gin palace' thus qualifying for a place in the Dublin Corporation to which – like his cheques – he was returned. [He was] elected to stop jobbery but only succeeded in stopping brickbats and found sticking plaster an admirable cosmetic.
>
> Having drawn on his account in the Post Office Savings Bank and after a number of visits to the South Circular Road, he in 'Jew' course opened a bungery of his own [and] monopolised ends of columns in the 'Saturday Pink', much to the annoyance of the Beecham's pill proprietors.

Many of the satirical criticisms of Alfie were above a pseudonym 'Oscar'. Alfie became an Alderman in 1913 and Oscar satirised him, telling how Byrne produced a melodrama called 'The Private Secretary' and how, during 'Fireball' Carson's march to Cork:

> Councillor Byrne's bar passed into the hands of the invaders. Here he did yeoman's service in his country's cause for one round of his nectar proved more effective than several rounds of grapeshot. For this and other signal services he was, on the opening of the College Green Parliament, accorded a peerage, taking the title of Lord Verdon de Talbo. Arms: on a shield vert a keg of Guinness rampant; Crest: a jar of J. J. & S. proper. Motto: 'Beer is thicker than water – slightly'.

With black humour, Oscar described Alfie's 'death' after a caucus meeting in Wynn's Hotel and parodied Kipling's poem *Gunga Din*:

> *Oh Bung! Bung! Bung!*
> *The angel host we know you are among.*
> *We have drunk your beer and paid you;*
> *'Twas our tuppences that made you,*
> *But we're better men than you are, Mr Bung.*

The publication was charged with libel by one Bill Richardson TC and in a scathing retort, it said:

> Bill Richardson [is] Alfy Byrne's (Bung, Talbot Street) political corner boy. Richardson's son got a job in the Corporation and his wife is seeking a job as a caretaker in the Morgue ...
> We know that Alfy Byrne's bungery, the Verdon bar, was used as a committee room ... that Alfy had personation agents and canvassers' money [and] that free drink was given away *ad lib*.

Privately and sometimes publicly, people resented Alfie's dapper appearance and his ready humour. These claimed him to be hypocritical but none could deny the thoughtfulness and industry he applied to the task of furthering his constituents' interests. Slum clearance and re-housing of the poor were his priorities. He opposed a concept of 'model homes' and advocated the building of flats at or near former inner-city housing sites. This and his unfailing rapport made him extremely popular with the poor of Dublin.

Alfie took considerable abuse when he supported John Kavanagh, Nationalist candidate for the North Dock Ward in 1913. *The Worker*, still berated him, called him 'the publican and the sinner – the one and only Alfy Byrne – with his head beautifully and artistically decorated with unnecessary plaster'. The publication's satirical manner continued and on 11 January 1913 an editorial warned:

> By the way, Alf, we will give you the same dose your
> blackleg tools got. Let us have [your] resignation [from the
> Corporation], Doggy Byrne and no equivocation.

Stones were hurled at Alfie when he arose to make an
election speech. One struck him on the forehead and he
collapsed afterwards and needed medical attention. Despite allegations against him, Alfie was a hard worker on
behalf of constituents. Some of his ideas were novel,
others downright amusing. He campaigned for the inclusion of tea as well as cocoa in the diet of children on the
Outdoor Relief list. Unions or workhouses, he felt, were
undignified and could be replaced by opening up
Kilmainham Jail or a disused military barracks in Thomas Street. A ladies' committee could run them, charging
4/6d for board and lodgings. As early as 1913 Alfie campaigned to have the names of the city's bridges named
after Irishmen. When Jim Larkin sought the use of the
Round Room of the Mansion House to explain his strike
strategy to the citizens of Dublin, Alfie displayed his ast-
uteness. He did not actually refuse the premises, but disagreed with a public meeting being the best method of
disseminating the facts. Larkin signed a complaint that
appeared in the *Evening Telegraph* and Alfie duly wrote to
the newspaper saying it was a forgery and that half the
names that appeared under it were obtained by fraud.
When Alfie praised the opening of a new city-centre playground and garden, the *Irish Worker* resumed its pun-
riddled pieces. One was introduced thus:

> Dear Mr Editor,
>
> Seeing by the daily press (*Daily Express* excluded) that Mr
> Alfie Bung T.C. (this does not 'stand' for teetotaller's com-
> panion) is endeavouring to turn the North Dock, which he
> so 'stoutly' misrepresents, into a veritable Garden of Eden

(please note, he does not sell cider) by his 'fill' anthropic
efforts to do good for his 'ale'ing constituents.

Alfie was accused by *The Toiler* of bowing and scraping
'for the sake of a few votes, to gutter bullies like Larkin
[and] Partridge and the other crowd of jail birds who
meet in the thieves' kitchen in Liberty Hall'. It was suggested that Alfie unearthed the celebrated document ad-
dressing Jim Larkin as 'Brother' and inviting him to a
meeting of Beaconsfield Orange Lodge (No. 337). This
was circulated with an accompanying flyer which asked
'Is Larkin tricking and swindling both Catholics and Pro-
testants?' The documents are carefully pasted into Alfie
Byrne's scrap book.[2]

On 16 January 1914, the *Irish Independent* reported an
outbreak of violence at three o'clock in the morning when
the election count for the North Dock Ward was completed. Friends had persuaded Alfie to run for Parliament. He asked them to draw up an election speech,
valued his property and sold it – on the assumption that
he would win the seat, which he did!

Some shots were fired that night too but the most
excitement was occasioned by Alfie's getting out of the
polling station by scaling the high railings. The gate was
locked, guarded by police and crushed against by the
crowd hailing their hero. Alfie Byrne became Member of
Parliament for the Harbour Division of Dublin, serving
from 1914 to 1918. In the December election of that year
Sinn Féin overwhelmed Redmond's Irish Parliamentar-
ians.

Alfie was a TD for the Mid-Division of Dublin from
1922 to 1923. He represented North Dublin and Dublin
North-East from 1923 to 1928 and from 1932 to 1951. He
topped the poll on many occasions and was twice suspended for pressing for more information on topics that

the Chair considered to be adequately answered. Between his spells in the Dáil, he was a Senator. In 1930, Alfie began a nine year term as Lord Mayor of Dublin and it is of his time in that office that most of the roguish tales are told.

One of the highlights of that period was the thirty-first Eucharistic Congress of 1932. Alfie was in his element introducing the members of the Corporation in public to the Papal Legate, Cardinal Lorenzo Lauri as he landed in Kingstown (Dun Laoghaire).

He could attend four functions in one evening and still pressed for schemes to assist the unemployed and destitute. So well known was he that after one re-election to Mayor, a newspaper illustrated its report with just a bowler and cane – Alfie's trademark.

Before the 1933 election, Alfie Byrne, ostensibly an Independent TD, was pro-Cumann na nGaedheal. At the end of December 1932, Senator Arthur Vincent had appealed to W.T. Cosgrave and his party and to Frank McDermott (Roscommon Independent deputy, Farmers and Ratepayers League) who had just formed the National Centre Party. Vincent wanted them to combine and form a new party. When the press reported this Alfie was quoted as having something bigger in mind. He aroused speculation by remaining reticent about his 'much wider [proposals]' which he believed 'would have the support of the vast majority of the Irish people'.[3] This was, in effect, the unification of political action among all who accepted the Commonwealth basis. A meeting held in the Mansion House on 29 December attracted 130 representatives from the professional classes, leaders of industry, very few labourers and 'farmers on a large scale with interests in the city'. Alfie's idea was to form a political party of the Irish Free State which would unify all opinions which recognised that the State's interests were

bound up within the Commonwealth of Nations, subscribed to by the Treaty of 1922.

Blustering about his grand scheme, Alfie caused a
laugh when he spoke about one party believing 'in having another round with England' as if he was speaking
about drink. Cumann na nGaedheal, he said, believed in
creating good will and good feeling with 'our best cust-
omer – in fact our only market'.

Cosgrave rose to the bait, pronouncing the plan as
having 'great potentialities for the country'. Whatever
enthusiasm was aroused became effectively scuttled
when Eamon de Valera called a sudden election. Alfie ran
and his election literature demonstrated his usual flair. It
contained a letter from the President, W.T. Cosgrave,
pointing out that the country was in such a serious state
that maximum confidence in its leaders was needed. 'In a
singular manner, you have won and held that confidence', said the letter. The President knew Alfie objected to
running for a Dáil seat but 'present circumstances are
such as to render it imperative in the national interest'
that he should run, despite the great personal sacrifice it
would incur. Impeccably groomed, wearing his chain of
office, Alfie stared out from above his own letter which
said: 'my slanderers are at work, lying tongues are busy.
Who are they? One of them from Belfast declared more
than once his admiration for the Communists.'

'We have had an overdose of catch-cries,' screamed
Alfie's leaflets as he added, 'Bread and butter and something to pay the rent is more important.' His confidence
in the intelligence of the electorate was minimal, obviously, for he went to remarkable lengths to explain how to
give him a first preference vote. 'You will be handed a
paper with my name near the top – like this.' [The box
with BYRNE Alfred was arrowed.] 'See that empty space?
Please fill it in, like that'. [Another bold arrow pointed the

way.]

Yet another hand-out told of his achievements – three years representing Dublin Harbour Division in the British House of Commons, member of the House of Commons Committee that had the old age pension increased from five shillings to seven and from seven to ten. As Lord Mayor he had kept hundreds of employees in work and had answered 7,000 letters dealing with cases of attempted conscription of Irishmen in Great Britain. He said: 'I wrote and published free to Irishmen in Great Britain, 10,000 copies of my book on the Conscription Acts ... my efforts were appreciated in Rome when attempts were made to conscript the students under the Allied regulations. I defeated the attempt,' he boldly proclaimed and Mr O'Riordan, Rector praised him saying, 'You certainly mean business when you undertake an important task.' A letter from Michael Collins in South Camp, Frongoch, dated 24 November 1916 was included. It requested Alfie to get publicity for the condition of Easter Week prisoners held there. On and on went the accolades. An excerpt from Dáil Reports told how the Minister for Defence, Mr Hughes declared, 'I think everyone with a peculiar case must go to Deputy Byrne, because I do not find them coming from anyone else.' Then Alfie listed his 'Peculiar Cases'; compensation for soldiers killed, maimed, mentally affected and for 'widows of volunteers and soldiers who died as a result of exposure during the troubled period'!

Alfie's support for Germany was noted in 1934 by the *Irish Workers' Voice*:

[The Nazis] took over the Metropole last week for another dance graced by von Kuhlmann, Séan MacEntee and Alfie. And the Tricolour and the Swastika of the fascist murder gang were draped in unholy matrimony in the ballroom.

King George V died in 1936 and Alfie attended his funeral. His opponents in the next election fought him on the issue but he was returned with a larger vote. When the office of President of Ireland was created by the 1937 Constitution, Alfie, then residing at 48 Palmerston Road, was early in the field as a candidate. He withdrew from the race when Dr Douglas Hyde *(An Craoibhin Aoibhinn)* was selected unanimously by all the Dáil parties. In the election of that year he polled 12,063 first preferences in the Dublin North-East constituency, compared with 9,693 for Oscar Traynor, a formidable opponent. His son, Alfred Patrick was first elected to the Dáil in the same election, polling 9,030 first preferences and coming second to Seán T. O'Kelly.

When Dublin's first female Lord Mayor, Kathleen Clarke – wife of 1916 revolutionary Tom, took over the Mansion House from Alfie in 1939 she removed the large painting of Queen Victoria from the foyer. She hired men to come at 6 am to carry out the removal and stayed up all night with her sister waiting for them. She removed other portraits of British royalty from other rooms. Alfie would not have approved![4]

Following a visit to Rome for the Holy Year in 1951, Alfie was created a Knight of the Grand Cross of St Sylvester and was granted a private audience by Pope Pius .

During 1954 and 1955, Alfie was again Lord Mayor of Dublin, thus completing an unique record in local government. The man who was said to have warmed the hand of every citizen of the city became known as 'The Shaking Hand of Dublin' and as such was a feature of *Dublin Opinion* cartoons, depicted extending an elongated hand, the politician's tool of trade. He found his way into a popular song too, replacing the Prince of Wales in:

Sure Alfie Byrne came up to me and shook me by the hand

Said he 'I've never heard the likes of MacNamara's Band.'

In a Queen's Theatre comedy sketch, Harry O' Don-ovan asked Jimmy O'Dea what kind of car he owned. The celebrated comedian answered: 'I used to have an Alfa Romeo but I've been shaking hands with the starting-handle so long, it's more like an Alfie Byrnio.' In July 1955, the degree of Doctor of Laws *honoris causa* was conferred by Dublin University. The citation read:

> We welcome Alderman Byrne, who has held the office of Lord Mayor more frequently than any other man, whose name is linked all over the world with Dublin; the champ-ion of the poor and needy, a friend of all men.

Friend of all men? Why then his inclusion in a book of rogues and scoundrels?

Because his old world courtesy was a political sham? Or was he a high-pressure public relations expert before his time? Did he perhaps fool the educated commentators by appearing to be a sham? A sort of Catch 22 Rogue or Honourable, honorary rascal?

Father of seven children, three of them Dáil deputies, last survivor of the Irish Parliamentary Party at West-minster, Alfie Byrne died on 13 March 1956. The *Irish Times* accorded him a glowing leader. 3,000 people tried to gain admission to the Pro-Cathedral. Dublin's streets were thronged for the funeral at which church and state were fully represented. Tributes came from all quarters. Were they or his critics wrong?

5

'GERMANY CALLING!'

Like another famous Irishman, William Joyce (1906–46) was born in Brooklyn, at 1377 Herkimer Street, on 23 April 1906. His father was Michael Francis Joyce who had married Gertrude Emily Brooke from Shaw, Lancashire at All Saints Church, New York on 2 May the previous year. It is important to note that Michael was born in The Neale, near Ballinrobe, Co Mayo around 1870, emigrated to the United States in 1888, filed a declaration of intent to become an American citizen on 22 July 1892 and became a naturalised citizen on 25 October 1894.

The family moved to Ireland in 1909 and lived for a time in Mayo before settling at 1 Rutledge Terrace in Salthill, Galway (some commentators place the arrival from Brooklyn, New York at 1914). William was educated at the Jesuit college of St Ignatius. A schoolmate, William Naughton, remembered him as a precocious lad who would ask, 'Are you Napoleon French?' in a strong, aggressive voice that was nasal almost to the extent of snorting. Unlike other lads, he would advise parents to take care of their boys if they had colds or other slight illnesses. He advised Mrs Naughton one day: 'Do tell Billy to take care of himself; after all, one's health is one's most precious possession.' He had a full, round face, thin, fair hair, was short, chubby and not handsome. His eyes were piercing. 'Willy' Joyce was unwashed and untidy, with the soiled lining of his school-cap sticking out.

Joyce was not very fond of sport but he was extremely bright academically and was particularly good at French. He would claim later that he served 'with the irregular forces of the Crown, in an intelligence capacity, against the Irish guerrillas'. Being so young, perhaps he merely carried dipatches but William Naughton remembers him sitting in the cab of a Crossley tender and having his lunch with the 'Tans and Auxiliaries' at Lenaboy Castle in Taylor's Hill, where Fr Griffin was said to have been shot. Joyce sometimes produced a grenade or revolver in class, to the horror of his fellow students. Courageous, with a fierce temper, he owned a chemical set – rare enough in those days. Once, he asked young Naughton to place a lighted match on his palm, saying he would not flinch – but he did. Willy Joyce was boastful, and fancied himself as a strong-willed character. He had rows with schoolmates and called them 'Sinn Féiners'. He was photographed then in a group from the Holy Angels Sodality.

Around 1920, the Galway General Omnibus Company was formed and Willy's father became its manager. Young Joyce was a temporary conductor. William left Ireland in 1921 and the family followed a year later, by which time William had passed the London University matriculation examination. [Was it only coincidence that the movement of the Joyces to England coincided with the departure of the British from southern Ireland?] His English education included the study of science at Battersea Polytechnic and of English and Literature for four years at Birbeck College.

On 21 October 1922, Joyce applied for enrolment in the University of London Officer Training Corps, stating that he hoped to study with a view to being nominated by the university for a commission in the regular army. He quoted his experience against the 'Irish guerrillas' and added that he had a knowledge of squad and bayonet drill and musketry. Explaining the possible difficulty about being born in America he told how his forefathers all had high positions in the British army and how he had been assured by his Brigade Headquarters in Ireland that he possessed the same rights and privileges as a natural British subject. 'I can offer testimonials of my loyalty to the crown ... I am in no way connected with the United States', he said. The authorities checked out the information with Michael Joyce and William was enlisted. He served for four years until his graduation.

A week after his twenty-first birthday William Joyce married Hazel Kathleen Barr at Chelsea Register Office. He embarked upon a two-year post-graduate course in philology (1928–30) and studied psychology at King's College (1931–33). During that period he was assisting the Conservative Party and was making speeches on their behalf. Disillusioned with Tory policies, he joined the newly-formed British Union of Fascists of Sir Oswald Mosley. They campaigned, making radical speeches and carrying bludgeons which they often used, particularly against the Communists of the East End of London. In one fracas, Joyce's right cheek was slashed from mouth to ear by a razor and he carried the severe scar to the grave. Seeking a passport in 1933 he reiterated his British origins and claimed his place of birth as Rutledge Terrace, Galway. In December 1934, with Sir Oswald and others, Joyce was acquitted of a charge at Lewes assizes, before Justice Branson and a jury, for riotous assembly at Worthing.

Joyce's marriage was dissolved in 1936. On 13 February of the following year he married Margaret Cairns White, a fellow-member of the Fascist movement, at Kensington Register Office. In that year too, he was expelled from Mosley's organisation. He directed his efforts instead to playing a leading role in the founding of the pro-Hitler British National Socialist League. It was alleged that they had an office and shop at Park Street, Bristol, where knives, truncheons and other weapons could be purchased. Joyce faced charges twice but was acquitted. He wrote seditious articles, pamphlets and a book, *National Socialism Now* (London 1937).

As war-clouds gathered he again claimed British citizenship, obtaining a passport in 1938. This was to prove a serious blunder. He went to Germany and on 18 September 1939, a few days after World War Two began, the *Daily Express* reported that Mosley's former lieutenant was broadcasting propaganda messages from Germany, using a posh, upper-class British accent. Likening it to the 'haw-hawing' tones of Norman Baillie Stewart, another English language broadcaster from Germany and former subaltern of the Seafort Highlanders, the writer bestowed on William Joyce a nickname that was to become a household word in Europe – Lord Haw-Haw.

Irish wireless owners seldom missed a Lord Haw-Haw broadcast as they followed the course of the war. They did not realise that coded messages were frequently delivered. An unidentified voice would introduce the programme. 'Germany Calling! Germany Calling! Here are the stations: Calais 514 metres, Breslau 316 metres, Cologne 456 metres, Luxembourg 1293 metres and the short-wave transmitter DXX 48.86 metres. And now here is William Joyce at the microphone to give "Views on the News".' The German prepared scripts amused many listeners for they included phrases like 'Honest Injun' believing them to be British colloquialisms. Their object was the undermining of the credibility of the censored British news services but the Jews and plutocracy received their share of abuse too. The main target of Lord Haw-Haw's barbs was, however, Winston Churchill. His talents, in the absence of comprehensive war news from the BBC and the national press, earned him a huge audience. A

New Year's Day survey in 1940 (a mere three months after his broadcasts began) estimated that a sixth of the listening public (about six million) tuned in to his programmes; and those figures excluded Ireland! Another eighteen million were occasional listeners.

Lord Haw-Haw's rumours were not cited as the reason, but a Government clamp-down on gossip was launched on 6 February 1940 with the distribution of 2,500,000 posters to offices, barber shops, hotels, bars, banks and public buildings. The dangers of loose talk formed the theme and artists depicted Hitler hiding under bus seats, on luggage racks or at bar counters. By the end of the month, Joyce's British audiences had dropped considerably and the Germans opened another news service called The New British Broadcasting Station, but it never captured the public imagination. It did cause mild hysteria in May 1940, however, when fears of a German invasion of England were whipped up to such an extent that a mid-June pamphlet offered the dubious advice: 'Most of you know your policemen and your ARP wardens by sight. If you keep your heads you will also tell whether a military officer is really British or is only pretending to be so.'[1] The NBRS promptly informed the public that the invading German parachutists would be dressed as miners!

Joyce's broadcasts were entertaining, yet impressive. His delivery was superb, his mimicking of Churchill masterly. A book of his, *Twilight over Europe* (Berlin 1940), sold 100,000 copies. It was written in German and in English. The importance of propaganda had already been established in the impression made on the French by Paul Ferdonnet's broadcasts from Stuttgart during the early months of the war. German bulletins aimed at the Belgian and Dutch armies were extremely effective also. Lord Haw-Haw became Germany's main broadcaster in English but he also enlisted traitorous prisoners of war and groomed them for other stations that claimed to be operating in Britain. Radio Caledonia targeted Scottish separatists. The Christian Peace Movement urged pacifism and the Workers' Challenge exhorted anti-employer action. Joyce's salary was 1,200 reich marks per annum.

Whenever Germany called, Lord Haw-Haw invariably disseminated some accurate piece of information about something mundane. This brought him an undeserved reputation for controlling an underground movement in Britain and many would believe any rumour as long as it was prefaced with 'Lord Haw-Haw said'. In Wolverhampton one evening a public clock stopped at 8.56. Joyce announced the minutia on his 9.15pm news. In another town, it was alleged that he correctly informed his listeners that their clock was fifteen minutes slow. This type of situation was bound to make people uneasy, so when Joyce forecast that a midland factory would be bombed shortly and that those painting it should not bother to finish the job, the painting contractors fled and were joined by workers. It was, of course, a munitions factory. Winston Churchill himself had to take action in July by ordering the civil service and the forces to 'check and rebuke expressions of loose and ill-digested opinion in their circle'.[2] He also advised that errant subordinates should be reported to the authorities or dismissed. The celebrated poster with Hitler and Goering sitting behind two old ladies in a bus, appeared around this time. 'Careless Talk Costs Lives' was the caption that became a slogan for 'Miss Leaky Mouth', 'Mr Pride in Prophesy' and 'Miss Teacup Whisper'. So it continued and William Joyce, by then a German citizen was awarded the Kriegsverdienstkreuz 1. Klasse (Cross of War – Merit of the First Class), a civilian honour, by Adolf Hitler. The citation described him as 'Chief Commentator, William Joyce'. His flamboyant 'Views on the News' expressed the utmost confidence in Germany's victory, even when the war was turning against them. In April 1945, the Russian and United States armies met at the Elbe, Berlin was surrounded and the German armies in Italy surrendered.

At the end of the month Adolf Hitler and his former mistress, wife of one day, Eva Braun, committed suicide. Lord Haw-Haw went on the air for the last time; he was drunk. 'Germany calling! Germany calling from Hamburg! You may not hear from me again for a few months ...' Later (21 April 1974) *The Sunday Times* would describe how 'the posh accent had disintegrated into a curious mix of father's Mayo brogue and mother's Upper Lancashire'. Thumps like those of a schnapps glass being hammered on a table emphasised points. 'No coercion, no oppression, no (thump) measures of tyranny that any foreign power can introduce will shatter Germany ... *Es lebe Deutschland! Heil Hitler!* And farewell!' he said.

The Nazi propaganda minister Joseph Goebbels made provision for Joyce's escape. On 28 May 1945, well-dressed and disguised, the broadcaster left his wife Margaret in a hotel and walked through a wood near Flensburg. He was close to the German border, beyond which lay Denmark and freedom. Two British officers, Captain Lickorish and Lieutenant Perry, were gathering timber and stumbled upon him. They challenged him, and when he answered, they recognised the voice of Lord Haw-Haw. Joyce's hand moved towards his pocket to produce his forged passport and one of the officers, thinking he was drawing a pistol, shot him in the thigh. He was unarmed and he insisted that he was Fritz Hansen. He was poorly rehearsed, however; the document claimed he was Wilhelm Hansen and a German permit which he carried showed he was William Joyce. Later, Margaret too was arrested and brought to a frontier-post to witness her husband being carried past on a stretcher.

He looked very pale and his face was sunken because he
was without false teeth ... he looked up and waved. Sum-
moning her wits to help him, she shouted desperately:
'Erin go breagh!' The message, 'Ireland for ever' was intended to suggest to him that he should claim to be Irish.
He gave no sign of hearing.[3]

Back in England, he was charged with high treason
and he faced a preliminary hearing at Bow Street. A curious public were accommodated by tenement-dwellers;
they admitted them to their quarters from which the yard
at the back of the station was visible. On 25 June 1945, the
trial began. Joyce insisted that he was not British but
American, before his defection. C.B.V. Head defended
him and produced a New York birth certificate. But his
false declarations in order to obtain a passport, his application for the OTC while at London University and other
instances when he claimed British citizenship were cited
by the prosecution. Besides, it was pointed out that the
mere taking of German citizenship during wartime was a
treasonable offence. After a short remand, Joyce was committed for trial.

Postponed to obtain evidence from America, the trial
eventually opened at the Old Bailey, London on 17 September 1945 before Lord Justice Sir Fredrick Tucker. The
indictment for high treason was read. The first count
charged that on 18 September 1939 and on other days between then and 29 May 1945, being a person owing
allegiance to the king and while a war was being carried
on by the German realm against the king, [he] did traitor-
ously adhere to the king's enemies in parts beyond the
seas – that is to say, in Germany – by broadcasting propaganda. The second count alleged that on 26 September
1940, Joyce purported to become naturalised as a subject
of Germany. The third count was similar to the first but

stipulated certain dates.

William Joyce's letters of application for the OTC at London University and for a passport were the main planks for the prosecution. Joyce had then stated that he was born in America of British parents, insisting that he was in no way connected with the United States and that he was prepared to 'draw the sword' against them or any other nation in Britain's interests. Joyce's defence was his American birth certificate. He claimed that he had been a good Conservative but had become disillusioned with their policies and, rather than become a conscientious objector, he left England to pursue his Fascist ideals and to propagate certain views, the expression of which would have been impossible in England during the war. Found guilty, William Joyce's case drew considerable comment. Many believed that the prosecution did not have a clear-cut case against him. Yet an appeal, heard before Lord Chief Justice Humphreys and Mr Justice Lynskey, was dismissed on 1 November 1945. Heard by the House of Lords between 10 and 13 December 1945, it failed again.

Prisoner No 3229 awaited the hangman's noose with decorum and patience. He was visited by his wife and others who found him resigned to his fate. After one of her visits, his wife received a letter expressing his love and impatience to have the execution over. He wrote a notice for publication which said:

> In death, as in this life, I defy the Jews who caused this last war; and I defy the Powers of Darkness which they represent. I warn the British people against the aggressive Imperialism of the Sowjet Union. I am prepared to die for my ideals; and I am sorry for the sons of Britain, who have died without knowing why.

The prison chaplain was welcomed and Joyce made his peace with God. He read a goodwill message from some of his former teachers at Birbeck College. He wrote a touching letter to his wife asking for a 'musical commemoration' and promising to do his best 'to send a wisp of my fleece – I've grown it since I was sentenced!' He told her to go to Galway and see the Spanish Arch, O'Brien's Bridge, Nile Lodge, Taylor's Hill, Leabeg Castle and 'above all – the stretch from Salthill to Blackrock'. In his last days, he said, he was near his boyhood again. 'I can see the injustice, the inequity of my non-political acts. I know my faults and am sorry that I have made others, you in particular, suffer'.[4]

On the morning of 3 January 1946, 300 people collected outside Wandsworth prison for the morbid privilege of reading the death notice when it would be displayed. Inside, Joyce received Holy Communion and spent some time in prayer before writing a final letter to his wife.

> I have just received Holy Communion and have prayed for you. This morning the spirit of St Pauli is strong upon me. I will not write much more. The letter which you left yesterday was the most marvellous I have ever received ... *Wir Haben doch gesiegt!*
>
> I salute you, Freja, as your lover forever. *Sieg Heil! Sieg Heil! Sieg Heil!*
>
> Your Will

The mathematical sign for infinity and a bracketed (Yp – Baa!), a reference to a private sheep game the couple played, were appended, then the time: 8.46.

While William Joyce was writing another letter, Mass was already being said for him by Very Rev. Fr Johnson, who knew him before the war, at Our Lady of Dolours' church in Fulham Road, London. Masses had begun in Crowthorne and in Galway too. All services were timed so that the Consecration would take place at the precise moment of Joyce's hanging.

Points of canon law had to be settled thirty years later, when Joyce's daughter arranged for his re-interment in Galway's new cemetery because William Joyce had received Anglican last rites after his execution. On 21 August 1976, Fr Lee celebrated a Mass in the cemetery church in a dignified ceremony attended by some relatives and a few Galwegians.

6

VICIOUS BUCK

Born of an aristocratic Norman family, Sir John Boyle Roche was a respectable Member of Parliament at the end of the eighteenth century, representing Tralee, Gowran, Portarlington and Old Leighlin in succession. A supporter of the establishment, he coined one bull in support of his alleged love for England and Ireland: 'I would have the two sisters embrace like one brother'. Another more celebrated statement was 'Posterity be damned! What has posterity done for us?' The skeleton in his cupboard was his younger brother, Tiger Roche, who attained the prerequisite for true roguery: while hated by some, he was held in the highest esteem by others.

Tiger was born in Dublin in 1729 and, like his brother, received a first-class education and grounding in the etiquette of good society. He made such an impression as a young gentleman that the Lord Lieutenant of Ireland, Lord Chesterfield, offered him a commission in the army. At the time, and although a mere sixteen years of age, he was then a member of the Dublin fraternity known as Bucks. These young blades led a high life, indulged in orgies and carousels and influenced each other greatly. Roche's group would not hear of him joining the army. The viceroy's offer would have suited a man of his temperament but he succumbed to his friends' wishes. Stubbornly, however, he rejected any other profession suggested, indeed he became quite vain and boasted about the rejected commission. For some years, he and his layabout associates indulged in all sorts of excesses and seemed to be everywhere that trouble brewed – almost in contradiction of his parliamentary brother, who said: 'No man can be in two places at once unless he is a bird'.

Tiger and his colleagues were involved in a drunken brawl one evening and a night-watchman attempted to quell the disturbance. The rioters turned their attention to the poor man and gave him such a beating that he died. The Bucks went to ground; Roche succeeded in making his way to Cork where he hid until a passage to America was arranged. After a spell working on the plantations, he eventually gave in to the urge for soldiering by joining the French army in their fight against the Indians. He distinguished himself in battle but witnessed great savagery and some of it rubbed off and he began to show the vicious streak that was to earn him his nickname.

His fickle and unprincipled behaviour nurtured among Dublin's Bucks left him with no qualms about deserting the French and joining the British forces. Here he was lionised for his intrepid spirit by his commanding officer, Colonel Massey, and his officers and soon he was offered a commission. This time he accepted eagerly. Soon he appeared to disgrace himself.

A brother-officer owned a magnificent fowling-piece which he valued greatly. Massey was informed that the weapon was seen in Roche's tent so he sent for the suspect and questioned him about the theft. Tiger denied having it so Massey ordered a search. The fowling-piece was found but Roche alleged that he purchased the gun from another Irish-born officer named Burke. Burke swore on his oath that Roche was lying so Tiger was charged with the theft and court-martialled.

Having nobody to speak in his favour, Roche had no defence. He was found guilty and dismissed with ignominy. Before the sentence was promulgated, he still protested his innocence and challenged the prosecuting officer to a duel. With the stiffest of upper lips Roche was told that being so disgraced he was not entitled to offer such a challenge, duelling being the recourse of gentlemen only. Infuriated by this insult, Roche followed the prosecuting officer to the parade ground and hurled insults at him. Then he turned on the camp guard commander, attacking him with his sword and vowing to kill him. The members of the guard jumped to their corporal's defence and disarmed Roche. Like so many cornered Indians he had seen, Roche sprang from a corner and fastened on the corporal's throat with his teeth. The victim screamed with pain and again his colleagues came to his rescue, dragging Roche from him. They succeeded in their efforts but Roche finished up with a mouthful of the corporal's flesh. There are claims that he swallowed it and proclaimed it the sweetest morsel he had ever tasted! It was this incident that earned him his nickname.

The British attack on Fort Carillon, Ticonderoga (8 July 1758) was imminent. Some reports say that Roche was retained for the battle and distinguished himself again, earning the praise of General Abercrombie, the expedition leader. It is said that but for the enormity with which the crime of robbery was regarded, the general would have re-instated him. Other accounts state that Roche was abandoned in the countryside and that he wandered aimlessly in the forests of New England until he met and befriended a group of Indians, reached Ticonderoga with them and joined in the celebrated battle.

In any event, the French won the day and Roche remained in New York state. He endured the rigours of abandonment, became ill and under-nourished. The governor of the state heard of his plight and his story. Because he believed in Roche's innocence, he helped arrange a passage to England with funds received by contacting some of Tiger's Dublin Bucks who had fared well.

The gratuity was ample and on reaching England Roche had enough money left to purchase a commission. On attempting to do so, the matter of the stolen fowling-piece came to light again and he was refused. Obsessed with what he considered a grave injustice, he tracked down the officer who had informed on him, a Captain Campbell. Roche went to the British Coffee-House, Charing Cross, and accused Campbell of calumniating him. Tempers rose, a duel was fought and both men received serious wounds.

On recovering, Roche embarked on an incredible crusade. In inns and assorted public places he voiced his complaint against military injustice and vowed to avenge himself on anyone discovered accusing him of the theft. In Green Park one day he met Colonel Massey and another officer. They had just returned from North America. Roche accosted them and again protested his innocence and beseeched them to take steps to clear his name. When they contemptuously refused, his tigerish instinct again surfaced; he drew his sword and attacked. He was no match for the pair so he decided to await a chance to meet either of them alone. This opportunity arose when he discovered that Massey's colleague was residing in Chester. He went there and walked the streets until he spotted him. Another duel took place but Roche's sword-arm was slashed and he had to retire.

Tiger Roche's name was cleared eventually. The former witness, Burke, was captured by a scalping party of Indians. Wounded seriously in the encounter and knowing that even if he survived the Indians would carry out their dire intent, he made a confession exonerating Tiger Roche. Burke had stolen the fowling-piece and had indeed sold it to Roche, who did not know its origin. By some means or other, word of the confession got back to

England. The army authorities checked its validity and were satisfied. Roche was granted a gratuitous commission.

The lieutenant who was wronged now witnessed officers and civilians doing everything in their power to make amends. His past was now his garland as socialites prevailed upon him to relate his experiences. Dublin called, however, and ensuring that the climate was right and that his murder charge was being overlooked in the face of his fame, he returned to the life of a better behaved Buck.

He was still handsome, he had been injured in a duel, he had fought with and against the Indians, the English and the French, he had refused to allow his improper conviction to carry on unchallenged, he even danced well – Dublin cherished its favourite son and it was only a matter of time before a young lady brought full respectability to Tiger by marrying him. As if to make amends for his previous misconduct in the city, Roche established what would nowadays be called a neighbourhood watch against the 'pinkwiddies' or 'sweaters' who were behaving much the same as the early Bucks. The city teemed with these miscreants who, although often of good parentage, had robbery as their main motive. They picked pockets or robbed by violence, pricking their victim's neck with the point of the sword which protruded from its scabbard and threatening them. Tiger's campaign began one night on Ormond Quay. He came across a group of the sword-wielding rabble attacking an old man and his family. Having rescued one lady who was screaming, he returned, took on the assailants single-handed and routed them. News of his gallant action spread and he availed of his popularity to form a group of army and civilian friends who would patrol the streets of Dublin at night and protect its citizens.

After the Treaty of Paris in 1763 the army was reduced. Roche retired and returned to his roguish ways. He squandered his wife's fortune and she left him but he continued carousing, fighting and indulging in all sorts of immoral vices. Heavily in debt, he absconded to London once more. An affair with a Miss Pitt, who had a fortune of £4,000 gave him opportunity for more extravagant living but his debts still grew and eventually he was arrested and imprisoned.

Prison life had a detrimental effect on Tiger Roche. Confined, unable to vent his anger on inmates, watched, bullied and subjected to ignominies, his spirit broke and he became a fawning, pathetic creature. Where previously his hackles were raised by insults, now he suffered them without complaint. Fellow prisoners who knew of his daring record taunted him and jeered when he refused to be baited. A notorious Irish Buck called English served a sentence in the same prison, allegedly for killing a waiter in a restaurant and demanding that £50 be put on the bill for the establishment's loss of an employee. English and Roche had disagreed in their young days and the former attacked Tiger one day. Roche cowered and wept as he endured a ferocious beating. The tiger had turned into a mouse.

Receipt of a legacy enabled him to pay off enough debts to get a release however, and he reverted to his deplorable conduct. More than ever he displayed arrogance and ill-temper. Unable to take any more beatings, Miss Pitt left him and he roamed the city's snooker halls and inns, insulting people. Incredibly, he was asked to stand for election in the Middlesex constituency. Some reports suggest that he declined because of receiving a large sum of money from supporters of another potential candidate, Colonel Luttrell, reputed betrayer of King James. (As it turned out, Luttrell lost the election to a candidate called

Wilkes, yet the Cabinet had him named Middlesex representative. This was later revoked.)

Roche fought another duel about this time and he displayed some untypical pity when he overcame a pair of attackers in Chelsea. One fired a pistol and the bullet grazed Roche's face; the other fled when Roche pinned the bad marksman to the wall. The couple were brought to justice and received a sentence of hanging but Tiger requested that their lives be spared, so they were transported.

Another young lady fell for Tiger, another large fortune was spent before Roche became a Captain of Foot and was posted to East India. On board the *Vansittart*, in which he set sail in the summer of 1773, his behaviour got him expelled from the captain's table and he was banished to the crew's quarters. They endured his rantings about the ship's captain, Ferguson, and the company at his table. Later, a sailor attested that he heard Roche threaten to shorten the race of Fergusons. When the ship docked at Cape Town, Ferguson went to his lodgings. At dinner that evening, he was called outside and when he did not return, a guest went to investigate. Ferguson was dead.

Suspicion fell upon Roche, because he had been seen in the neighbourhood before the murder. So he fled to the bush and lived for a while in a native village. The outcome of this affair is shrouded in contradictions. Some say the Dutch authorities tried Roche and acquitted him. More dramatic accounts describe his being 'broken alive upon the wheel'[1] or suggest suicide. The acquittal seems to have taken place, however, for Roche continued on to Bombay on board a French vessel. The British administration there had been informed of the Ferguson murder so they arrested Tiger. He pleaded previous acquittal, adding that even if he had committed the offence, it was done outside British jurisdiction. But he was held in custody and later returned to England to stand trial. Baron Burland heard the case at the Old Bailey on 11 December 1775.

Evidence described Ferguson getting a message, strapping on his sword, taking a loaded cane and leaving his lodgings. A guest called Grant followed him, saw Roche for a brief instant, then heard a clash of blades. Grant claimed he saw Roche leaving the scene and Ferguson being carried inside. He had nine wounds on the left, unguarded, side.

Roche's threat issued among the *Vansittart* sailors was quoted. The prosecution asked why Roche should wander about in a strange port and be lurking about the home of one against whom he had issued threats. They described the cowardly attack on Ferguson's unguarded side but witnesses differed when it came to quoting the exact message brought to Ferguson asking him to come out.

Defending himself again, Tiger said he asked a young native to show him around the town. They were followed by someone who disappeared when they approached Ferguson's lodgings. Immediately, Roche was felled by a heavy blow from a loaded stick. Rising with difficulty, for his arm was dislocated from the fall, he took on his assailant, Ferguson. He admitted to killing the captain – but in self-defence. The boy who accompanied Roche that night gave corroborative evidence, as did one sailor. Roche's suggestion was that Ferguson was having him watched with a view to killing him and that one version of the message brought to Ferguson suggested it was a signal that Roche was outside. Ferguson's wounds were on the left side simply because he used the cane to parry Roche's thrusts to the right.

Tiger Roche was acquitted but London society had had its fill of the argumentative, bad-tempered, brutal,

impecunious vagabond who 'regarded swords no more
than knitting needles, and pinked every man he faced in
combat'[2] – a rogue in the very worst sense of the word.
Anyway, his age mitigated against continuing as a Buck.
He returned to India and was forgotten.

7

THE GORGEOUS GAEL

Guardsman, fighter, wrestler, ladies' man, singer, movie-star, drinker, raconteur, jailbird, likable rascal one day, villain the next – Jack Doyle's claim to roguery is as strong as a pint of porter. He was born on 31 August 1913 at Queen Street in the port of Cork once known as Cove. Called Queenstown for a while it later preferred the Irish form – Cobh.

First called Joe, he was second child of Mick and Anastasia, who also had children called Bridie, Betty, Bill, Mick and Tim. Mick, nicknamed 'Nelson', was a seaman, whose brother was a British Navy boxing champion. He fought himself too, but with little success. He wanted one of his sons to be a boxer or a priest, until he suffered a series of accidents that left him disabled and poor.

Young Joe was always the 'hard-chaw'. He cheated at pitch-and-toss and was extremely extrovert – performing outlandish feats to attract attention; like eating raw turnips or eggs, drinking bottles of medicine that others hated or exposing himself to young girls. He stole from shops by asking for something he knew was kept out the back; when the shopkeeper went out, Joe used a stick with a hook to lift items from the shelves. Being tall for his age, he could jump up and steal a ham too. Charged with robbing a pair of ducks, he was found guilty, but let off with a warning. A popular lad, Joe became a hero for beating older bullies in fist-fights. He fought with stones and catapults too and frequented the local soldiers' and sailors' hostel.

After mitching from school and robbing an orchard at the age of twelve, Joe and his pals were accosted by a vigilant adult who tried to march them back to the school. Joe attacked the man and beat him up. So ended his schooldays.

Doyle worked the coal boats or helped liner passengers by carrying their luggage. For a while he used his Confirmation name Alphonsus. He was tall, well built, handsome and, even at fourteen years of age, popular with female Americans! Like many another youth of his time he read a book by Jack Dempsey who had been world heavyweight boxing champion from 1919 to 1926 and had just been defeated in the famous 'long count', by Gene Tunney. Unlike them, however, Joe had the ability to fight; he took on the toughest dockers and won. Local reports say he nearly killed an ass with a punch.

A man called Tim McCarthy noticed the potential of this fifteen-year-old, 180 pound, six-footer. Failing to get him fights because of his youth, Tim suggested the army as a career which would afford him a chance of recognition. The new National Army turned him down on age grounds so he sailed to Pembroke, joined the Irish Guards and began using the name of his world champion hero. Jack Doyle found the discipline difficult, felt homesick yet entertained the lads in his billet by singing Irish ballads.

In the depot gymnasium at Caterham he tried his right-hand punch that he had been practising alone; his instructor fell, as did his first amateur opponent. Doyle was on his way and he knew it! He regaled girls with predictions of becoming a boxing champion and seldom allowed another man to share the limelight. On completion of his training, Jack was posted to the Palace Guard, stationed at Victoria, London. There he concocted stories about the behaviour of royalty which he claimed to have noticed while on guard duty, tales with which he amused customers in the city pubs – when he was not brawling! City life appealed to him, not least because of its access to professional boxers. He sparred with Len Harvey, British middleweight champion and realised that boxing was far different from brawling. But he impressed the champion who recommended him to manager, Daniel Sullivan. Sullivan helped obtain Doyle's discharge by purchase.

Before he left the army in February 1932, Jack Doyle fought for his regiment in the army finals and kept his undefeated record intact. He sang 'The Dear Little Town in the Old County Down' for his mates before leaving for a world of fast cars, faster women, fan mail and fame. Impeccably groomed and sporting a red carnation in his buttonhole, his dark, wavy hair and fine physique were impressive. His first five professional fights were won by knockout while he himself was a knockout with elegant women in fashionable restaurants. His first major conquest was Phyllis Kempton, wife of a racehorse and greyhound-owner whose string included Mick-the-Miller. Sullivan encouraged Doyle's womanising; it was good for business. He did not reckon on the Corkman's capacity for sexual activities.

So far, however, Doyle's hectic socialising was not affecting his boxing. Between August and November 1932, he had knocked out four more opponents in the first or second round. Under new management in 1933 he won against Jack Humbeek but was disqualified in his first attempt at the British Heavyweight Title. The first fight was preceded by intensive training under Francois Descamps, George Carpentier's mentor, in France. Doyle took a fancy to Descamp's daughter, Denise. A French chaperone saw to it that the relationship would be confined to Jack singing Irish ballads in return for the 'Marseillaise' from mademoiselle. Jack learned little about boxing, however and he remained a fighter. Yet he tried to exercise what he had learned in the fight against Humbeek but had to abandon it for fear of losing.

Before the title fight, Doyle sang at the London Palladium and recorded his celebrated 'Mother Machree' on the Decca label. There have been suggestions that a prostitute was paid handsomely to bed Doyle after a drinking session so that he would contact a venereal disease. These rumours were fanned when the fight was postponed so that Doyle could receive treatment in hospital, allegedly for a back injury.

White City Stadium was packed for the occasion. Doyle claimed that he received a good-luck telegram from Jack Dempsey; he ensured a contract by which he would receive £3,000 – win, lose or draw. In the event he was disqualified in the second round, for a low punch. Worse, his purse was withheld and the British Boxing Board of Control allowed him only £260 – to be divided with his mother, whose poor circumstances he had pleaded. He was also suspended for six months.

To help finance a court case, Doyle sang in Dublin's Theatre Royal for four weeks and in Cork's Opera House where he received a returned hero's welcome. He cut more records too. Roger Casement's defence counsel, KC Sergeant Sullivan was engaged for an action against the BBBC's right to fine and suspend him, which was successful. But Jack could not celebrate because he was in training – seriously this time – for a comeback. It paid off and he knocked out Frank Borrington in the first round on 19 March 1934. Financial arguments with his management caused his departure from the ring for a concert tour. An appeal by the BBBC went against him and he again lost the £3,000 from the Peterson fight. Disgusted, he went home to Cork and had a huge party.

In 1935, Doyle relished a film role based on a real-life roguish buccaneer. *McGluskey the Sea Rover* should have been a Scot, but became a Corkonian to suit the Gorgeous Gael. He flirted with its female stars but celebrities like Gertrude Lawrence and Jessie Matthews welcomed the handsome hunk too. Walter Friedman promised training from Doyle's hero, Jack Dempsey, and became his manager. When Wallis Simpson stole the Prince of Wales from Lady Thelma Furness, Jack Doyle consoled the loser in St Moritz, before leaving for the United States where he was convinced he would be successful. Being just twenty-one years of age, handsome and ambitious he had a good try. Jack Dempsey was more interested in Irish stew at his new restaurant than in smiling Irish eyes so he offered little assistance. Undaunted, Jack let the American public know that he was set on taking on Max Baer, the world champion in the ring and Marlene Dietrich and others on the screen. He took on Baer in other ways too: escorting a former and current girlfriend of his! But he met and marred wealthy Hollywood star Judith Allen among screams from young fans calling for their 'Heart-Smasher', 'Hibernian Mocking-Bird'. Judith was divorced from world heavyweight wrestling champion, Gus Sonnenberg.

Doyle's new wife fired Friedman and financed further training. Jack knocked out three opponents in as many weeks during June–July 1935 but was beaten by a technical knockout at the hands of Buddy Baer, on 29 August. He had been caught napping, said his defenders, while throwing a kiss to Judith from the ring. With a little persuasion from the same lady, he quit boxing but then took to spending her money in ways that she did not like. In an attempt to heal wounds the pair toured in a show in which both of them featured. They brought it to England, but Jack still could not resist a young lady's advances and the relationship deteriorated. When the show came to the Theatre Royal, Jack was expecting a repeat of the previous rapturous welcome but, like Parnell, he was now married to a divorcee and Ireland was offended. The likable rogue had become an adulterer in his countrymen's eyes.

Back in England, he attempted to regain his boxing licence but he still owed the BBBC costs and his overtures were spurned. So the couple went back to Hollywood where Doyle played an officer in the film *Navy Spy*. He played his favourite role with the big names in Hollywood too and it is alleged that Clark Gable kept a friendly tally-card of Doyle's conquests – until his own girlfriend's name appeared on it!

The ring still called and he returned to England, alone. Before a fight at Wembley on 19 January 1937, Judith divorced him. His shock was compounded when, after hammering Alf Robinson in the opening round, he was disqualified for striking his opponent while he was on the ground. Not beyond striking a foul blow in other areas, he told reporters the most intimate details of his life with Judith, at the same time alleging that he wanted her back. And while he pined he was high-flying with a thirty-five year old aeronaut, Beryl Markham! During a short break in their passionate affair, Jack flew to California to beg Judith's forgiveness! He beat Harry Staal in the sixth round at Earl's Court in February and won on points against King Levinsky in August.

Speedboat queen, millionairess of the wealthy Dodge family, Delphine Godde played piano while Jack Doyle sang for her husband, Tim. By day he rode with her in Windsor Park and enjoyed sumptuous food and wine; he slipped down to her room at night. Never did a more unfit man step into the ring for as important a fight, yet he beat King Levinsky at Wembley on 27 April 1937, his first win going the distance.

Back in Godde's home, where he was now resident,

his attention turned to Delphine's fifteen-year-old daughter, Christine and Horace Dodge Junior's current wife, ex-Parisian Follies stunner, Mickey. Eventually, Doyle was asked to leave and Delphine's family prevailed on her to return to America. Fond of her money, Jack professed love but as soon as she cleared the Welsh coast he was consorting with glamorous, rich singing star, Libby Holman. An arranged fight fell through when he sailed with her, supposedly to obtain a divorce in Reno. By the time they docked, Libby had dumped Jack – so he sought out Delphine again, hoping she would divorce her husband and marry him. The Dodges were not having any of that, however. They paid Jack off with a handsome cheque (reported to be $50,000 and £100 per month for life) and told him never to follow Delphine again.

Doyle lost two fights against Eddie Phillips in 1938 and 1939. Of one, Fleet Street journalist Peter Wilson said in his book *Ringside Seat* (London 1948): 'I can't describe Doyle's transformation from the perpendicular to the horizontal better. What's more, his early Guard's training reasserted itself in this crisis, for he lay rigidly to attention while he was being counted out.' The two fights were marked by squabbles about money (Doyle sought advance payment of his purse) and another trip to the United States that enraged the Dodge family. Jack claimed it was to see Delphine, who was ill but there were allegations about his attempting to get another pay-off from the wealthy Anna Dodge by claiming she wrecked his relationship with Delphine. Charged with illegal entry via Canada, he was jailed in Los Angeles.

Mexican beauty, Movita, passed up a date with Howard Hughes to meet Jack Doyle who soon proposed to her. She accepted, but Jack was deported. His contacts served him well and when the ship called at El Salvador, he visited its president, whom he had met socially in London, and arranged for his return to Mexico. Doyle and Movita were married there in the New Year. Gambling debts mounted again, Doyle turned to England once more and so came his second defeat by Eddie Phillips, a knock-out in the first round.

As a world war was starting, Jack and Movita went on tour and became a popular act. It was said that he volunteered to re-join the Irish Guards and was told he was doing more good entertaining the hard-pressed British population. He became landlord of a Buckinghamshire public house, where he and his beautiful wife were happy for a while. He still wore the red carnation in his button-hole. Money problems persisted and the old pattern of brawls and booze recurred. People were getting fed up with Doyle but he had a plan to re-establish himself.

Knowing that the Irish people still resented his marriage to Judith Allen, he and Movita re-married in St Andrew's Church, Westland Row, then opened a show at the Theatre Royal. It was a sell-out so Irish boxing promoter, Gerald Egan matched Doyle with Chris Cole of Mullingar, the country's best heavyweight. The referee at Dalymount Park stopped the fight in the first round as Cole pummelled Doyle. The audience's fury was fanned by reports of Jack being drunk before the contest. The 'Gorgeous Gael' was feeling low and even a knock-out win against Butcher Howell two months later did not help; he decided it was to be his last fight. A tour of a stage show called 'Something in the Air' was successful, mainly because Movita had won Irish hearts. The pair's rendering of the Jimmy Kennedy song 'South of the Border' always drew applause. They lived in Dalkey, Movita all the time experiencing Jack's excesses. She finally left him in May 1945.

For assaulting a member of the Garda Siochána, Doyle was sent to Mountjoy for a fortnight. Many public-houses barred him. Down and out and homeless, he frequented the Seamen's Mission, Dolly Fawsett's, and late night cafes. Yet he tried still to project himself as a celebrity. After the war, a lady called Nancy Keogh took him in hand. He again sought his British boxing licence, was again refused, so he took up wrestling. His old rival Eddie Phillips was one of his opponents; Tony Galento and Butty Sugrue were others (Ireland's strong-man, Butty – himself a likely candidate for honorary roguery – had once promoted one of Jack's concerts). The 'Gorgeous Gael' name was struck for the mat game and Jack picked up plenty of money and more fans. He played a tiny role in the film *The Belles of St Trinian's*. When even these ring days ended, Doyle was reduced to singing in pubs and clubs. In 1966, Doyle was convicted for stealing cheese from a store. The pub-singing ended, he joined the dole-queue, accepted free drinks or unrepayable loans wherever he could find them. There were rumours of his receiving stipends from Movita and from the Dodge family – to keep away! By 1976, even his loyal Nancy must have had enough; she slipped away quietly. It was near the end of the road for the man who, magnificent in a camel hair coat had once strolled down O'Connell Street throwing coins to kids, had owned a racehorse and had mixed with the highest of London and New York society.

On 13 December 1978 Jack Doyle – Gorgeous Gael, Singing Thrush, Fighting Nightingale, Pugilistic Playboy, – died a pauper at St Mary's Hospital, Paddington, to where he had been removed from a seedy basement flat in Notting Hill Gate. His remains were returned to Cobh, where Cork's boxers placed a wreath fashioned in the shape of a boxing-glove. In his heyday he was a likable rogue but his escapades brought him infamy. His sad death, alone and penniless, brought him sympathy and forgiveness.

8

MADAMS OF MONTO

When the Czar of Roossia
And the King of Proosia
Landed in the Phoenix Park in a big balloon,
They asked the polis band to play 'The Wearin' o' the
Green'
But the buggers in the Depot didn't know the tune:
So they all went up to Monto, Monto, Monto,
Up to feckin' Monto, langaroo to you!

Ballads and stories were rendered in the streets of Dublin, a civic farewell was granted too one day in 1973 when northsiders marked the demolition of the Gloucester Diamond. It was the end of a legend – the destruction of which began in 1925 with a dawn 'morality raid' on the Kips of Monto – named after Montgomery Street, at their heart.

By the year 1610, author Barnaby Rich had spent forty-seven years in Ireland. In Dublin, he noted, there were numerous idle, lazy housewives called tavern keepers 'most of them well-known harlots'.[1] Indeed it was difficult to find any tavern without a harlot, he observed. The city's recorder, Mr Handcock, had a reputation for a knowledge of law and for being a bold and just magistrate. John Dunton, an eccentric English bookseller arrived in Dublin in 1698. He told how:

> many of the strolling courteous ladies of the town have by his orders been forced to expose their lily white skin down

76

to the waist at a cart's tail, by which he is become at once
the fear and hatred of the lewd, and love and satisfaction
of sober persons.[2]

In 1880 prostitutes accounted for 6.25% of inmates in
South Dublin Union Workhouses. This compared with
2.32% who were unskilled females![3] The aptly named Bull
Lane, on the south side near St Patrick's Cathedral boasted 200 prostitutes then. On the north side, however, the
trade had been flourishing since about 1825 and less than
a hundred years later, after the establishment of Saorstát
Éireann, it was often said: 'When the Senate is in session,
Monto is full'. Tales were told of husbands explaining
their absence to virtuous wives who heard that they had
frequented the premises of Becky Cooper, Mrs Hayes,
Mrs Sheppard, May Oblong, Meg Arnott or Annie Mack.
This 'fanfare of strumpets' represented a Dublin society
that terrorised Frank Duff's Legion of Mary and pleasured royalty, rebels and ribald roisterers. To the east of
fashionable Sackville Street (O'Connell Street) and only a
whiff of heady, cheap perfume away, ladies of Strumpet
City's red light night area plied their trade for close on a
century, in a brothel district that was among the most
licentious in Europe. The distinguished *Encyclopaedia
Britannica* considered Dublin's night-women more overt
than those of Algiers; as long as their business was conducted within certain unwritten confines, the police
seemed to turn a blind eye. Its closeness to the docks and
railway station drew visiting sailors and departing merchants. Methylated spirits were drunk and sometimes a
girl's body was found in the Liffey, perhaps brutally beat-
en. The cheaper women attracted business by walking the
streets dressed only in a raincoat which they flicked open
when a prospective client was noticed approaching. The
'Monto' area housed 1,600 in its heyday. The Hay Hotel,
Parnell Street, was so called because some hay was al-

ways kept on its window-sill for the horses of jarvies who drank inside, many of them waiting for their customers to return from the 'Kip'. Oliver St John Gogarty said of Monto: 'Here nothing but the English language was undefiled'.[4]

There was once a botanic garden in Mecklenburg Street. The architect James Gandon, who designed Dublin's Custom House and other beautiful buildings, lived there for a while. The sculptors Edward Smyth and John Foley resided in Montgomery Street, later called Foley Street, after the latter. But that was before 'Monto' became an area that James Joyce would call nighttown:

> ... before which stretches an uncobbled tramsiding set with skeletontracks, red and green will-o'-the-wisps and danger signals. Rows of flimsy houses with gaping doors. Rare lamps with faint rainbow fans. Round Rabaiotti's halted ice gondola stunted men and women squabble. They grab wafers between which are wedged lumps of coal and copper snow. Sucking, they scatter slowly. Children. The swancomb of the gondola, highreared, forges on through the murk, white and blue under a lighthouse. Whistles call and answer .... A deafmute idiot with goggle eyes, his shapeless mouth dribbling, jerks past, shaken in Saint Vitus' dance. A chain of children's hands imprisons him ... A pygmy woman swings on a rope slung between the railings.[5]

Joyce used the precise name of one of Monto's ladies, Bella Cohen, in his epic. Bella flaunted herself and her women alongside a 'midnight mission house' set up by Protestant churchmen to combat the vice in the area. Bella's house was far busier! Joyce described her:

> ... a massive whoremistress [,] dressed in a threequarter ivory gown, fringed round the hem with tasselled selvedge flirting a black horn fan like Minnie Hauck in *Carmen*. On her left hand are wedding and keeper rings. Her eyes are deeply carboned. She has a sprouting moustache.

Her olive face is heavy, slightly sweated and fullnosed, with orangetainted nostrils. She has large pendant beryl eardrops .... She glances around at the couples ... Her large fan winnows wind towards her heated face, neck and embonpoint. Her falcon eyes glitter.[6]

Every brothel operated around the clock; cheap, watered whiskey was available for patrons, many of them sailors brought by jaunting-cars from the docks. The madams' business cards were displayed on notice-boards in army barracks and discreet entry was guaranteed to all who wished to preserve anonymity. For the less reserved, madams' names were emblazoned on the fanlights above their front doors. The normal charge for entry to a high-class brothel was ten shillings (fifty-pence in today's currency). At least £5 was left by a prostitute's bed on departure. Some of the women rented rooms and paid ten shillings to the madam before leaving. Houses with single-figure numbers in Mecklenburg Street were open-door brothels; these were frequented by the common classes of the day.

Playwright and author Seamus de Burca described a typical Monto madam as being ample of bosom, ponderous of posterior, malodorous of perfume, belching with over-eating and, 'her corrugated neck was cemented and repaired with cheap powder; her button-like nose was dilated like a dog in a rut; and her small beady eyes shone in the gloom'.[7]

Becky Cooper was the last survivor of her trade in Monto. She claimed that her actual name was Mrs Rebecca Whittaker. Haughty to inferiors, she paid great deference to the high and mighty. Dressed in the manner of great beauties of her time – black, high-collared Bombazine – she fondled a cameo brooch depicting Aglaia, Thalia and Eurynome, the Three Charities. To confidantes, she explained how it was a gift from an establishment gentleman but unwelcome customers, especially young blades accompanied by their own women, were ejected by her kept man, James. Not for Becky the coarse offers of her competitors. She entertained her men in a genteel fashion and only at a late stage of their imbibing would she suggest that they might welcome the pleasure of one of her ladies.

Becky was not always in the upper league of madams, of course. She served her time in the open-door establishments and earned a place in a rude rhyme:

> *Italy's maids are fair to see;*
> *France's maids are willing*
> *Less expensive far, for me –*
> *Becky, for a shilling!*

Her good looks and charming manner earned her 'field work' at the annual Dublin Horse Show or at the Phoenix Park racecourse where she would solicit business discreetly on behalf of her madam.

In the early nineteenth century, Becky set up her own salon, which flourished. Of a generous nature, she shared her new-found fortunes with others and subscribed to a number of charities. Some of these contemptuously returned her subscriptions.

> *There goes Mrs Mack*
> *She keeps a house of imprudence;*
> *She has an old back parlour*
> *For poxy medical students.*

Mrs Annie Mack once owned up to eight or ten brothels in Mecklenburg Street, giving the area the nickname 'Mackstown'. She had not the good looks of Becky Cooper, being ruddy-complexioned, double-chinned and of mean countenance. She had a coarse laugh and was dictatorial to her clients, many of them medical students. A pianist played at her establishments. It was said that her girls were often physically punished by Annie's 'fancy men' (like today's 'bouncers') if they failed to tempt their clients to buy enough liquor on the premises. Annie Mack had considerable business acumen. Every time a new regiment arrived at the Royal Barracks, she presented her card to its commanding officer. Young officers then travelled in side-cars supplied by her. When she realised that her age would soon begin to tell, she established a costuming business for the prostitutes of Monto. If they were down on their luck she was not beyond lending them a little money – but at an exorbitant interest rate.

The strikingly beautiful Meg Arnott lived in a fashionable house in Mount Merrion and was able to send her daughter to an English finishing school. She believed in advertising, so she hired landaus and paraded her girls along the busy shopping streets where a raised eyebrow from one of them was enough to attract custom. Many of her young prostitutes came from good homes, attracted by the expensive clothes worn by the 'carriage girls'. Meg's clients were well-to-do and often treated their courtesans to a box in the theatre or a ball in the Metropole.

A persistent Dublin rumour linked the Prince of Wales, later Edward VII, with Meg Arnott's establishment. It was said that Meg arranged for an actress, Nellie Clifden, to be smuggled into his quarters in the Curragh Camp during the year 1861. Both as Prince and as King he visited Dublin and it was alleged that the underground passages to Monto and Meg's were used by him. At least one Monto prostitute graduated to pleasuring London's nobility. Her background suited her for the business, her father being bailiff for Lord Hertford, the Co. Antrim lecher who included courtesans in his party whenever he travelled. Her name was Laura Bell and from an early age she supplemented her shopgirl's wages by prostitution on Belfast's streets. Towards the middle of the nineteenth century she arrived in Dublin and took up the profession on a full-time basis. Personable and strikingly beautiful, she became quite wealthy. Her customers included Oscar Wilde's father, Sir William. She drove a four-wheeled, hooded carriage, pulled by two white horses, but did not seem to like Monto as she stayed there only a short while.

Laura became a full-time mistress to an Indian prince in London's fashionable Knightsbridge area. He gave her a magnificent home and all sorts of luxuries which were said to have cost in the region of £250,000. Around 1862, however, she married an army officer. About a decade later she seems to have suffered remorse, for she opened a mission house and travelled to preach at evangelical meetings.

Heavily made-up and wearing huge cameo earrings, May Oblong finds mention in Brendan Behan's *The Quare Fellow*:

> Ah where do you leave poor May? The Lord have mercy on her, wasn't I with her one night in the Digs, and there was a Member of Parliament there, and May after locking him in the back room and taking away his trousers, with him going over the North Wall that morning to vote for Home Rule. 'For the love of your country and mine,' he shouts under the door to May, 'give me back me trousers.'
>
> 'So I will,' says May, 'if you shove a fiver under the door' ... Ah, poor May, God help her, she was the heart of the roll ... when she was arrested for carrying on after curfew, the time of the Trouble, she was fined for having concealed about her person, two Thompson sub-machine guns, 1921 pattern, three Mills bombs, and a stick of dynamite ...[8]

Seamus de Burca's play, *The End of Mrs Oblong*, was first

staged in the Eagle Theatre, Glasthule on 14 August 1973. In its opening scene, May tells a visiting evangelist:

> I am a third generation prostitute. My mother used to tell me I had royal blood in me veins. You've heard about Eddy – King Edward? He was a bit of a one for the ladies. But to speak the truth he'd a wanted to be King Solomon to have all the women that claimed him. No, but I do believe my father was one of the viceregal boyos. I have a photograph of him autographed –'to the light of my lights' – romantic, wasn't it? You can't beat a bit of sentiment – in the right place at the right time of course [His] britches I remember were in the house for years and years – until the moths got at the fork. We never encouraged pimps. The madams were all capable of managing their establishments – no one could ever say one of the houses was misconducted. Unless the police misconducted themselves which they did on occasion to suit their own ends, for the purpose of seducing the girls or robbery or blackmail.[9]

During the dawn of the twentieth century, the police attempted to clean up 'The Kips'. Their persecution drove the prostitutes onto the streets and so certain people of influence prevailed on the authorities to leave the girls alone so that they would return to the brothels. The zealous Frank Duff, founder of the Legion of Mary, the Passionist priest, Fr Ignatius and others eventually tackled the problem. The death of a young prostitute from venereal disease coincided with their campaign, thus giving it considerable success. A Jesuit mission in the Pro-Cathedral during 1925 reinforced Duff's efforts. May Oblong sought a large pay-off to close her establishment. The names of similar hard-liners were given to the police and, supervised by Colonel Dave Neligan, they conducted a midnight raid on Monto. Only one madam underwent imprisonment as a result, but the area was cleared and the Jesuit mission concluded with a blessing of the houses and an adorning of each door with a holy picture. The

Digs, the Village, the Bad Place, the Kips, Monto – the names, like those of its inhabitants live on.

> *Where are the great Kip Bullies gone*
> *The Bookies and outrageous Whores*
> *Whom we so gaily rode upon*
> *When youth was mine and mine was yours ...*
>
> Gogarty

9

THE KERRY BOER

As they would say in Dunquin, Maurice Kavanagh was born within a stone's throw of the wild Atlantic Ocean and his lifetime was often as tempestuous as the wild seas that tossed themselves upon the Blaskets. He was born on 28 March 1894 and Báile na Rátha was his native townland; Muiris Caomhánach his name – for this was the heart of the Kerry Gaeltacht and like his neighbours, he spoke Irish every day. But neither the native or foreign forms of his Christian name was to stay long. During his schooldays, the Boer War was being fought and Paulus Kruger (1825–1904) was making a name for anti-British activities which included the purchase of arms from Germany to attack the Cape Colony and Natal in September 1899. In playground games in Dunquin, Muiris Ó Scanláin from Ghleann Loic led a 'company' in a series of attacks upon young Kavanagh's 'soldiers'. The schoolmaster joined in the fun and nicknamed Scanlon 'The Colonel', after Horatio Kitchener, the British strategist in South Africa. Maurice Kavanagh rejoiced in the title he received – 'Kruger'. It was to remain with him all his life.

Early in 1913, Kruger bade goodbye to his father, Seán Donal, his mother, Máire Seosamh, sister Peig and brothers Liam, Seamus and Seán. With other youths from Dunquin, he made his way to Springfield, Massachusetts. He attended Commercial High School and also spent a brief spell at Fordham University. On 27 May 1920, he became an American citizen. His address then was 66

Chestnut Street, Hartford, Connecticut and he was described as being five feet ten inches in height, fair of skin with brown eyes and hair.

Having worked with the firm of Berry & Sons in Hartford, Kruger became a gun-toting bodyguard to Eamon de Valera when, as President of the First Dáil, he visited America during 1919–20. Kavanagh was also the secretary and advance tour representative for the Irish tenor, Walter Scanlan. One of his duties was the auditioning of chorus-members for Scanlan's 'The Blarney Stone' show but phony Irish accents received a cold welcome. He became well known in theatres across America. As a member of the Irish Drama League and a drama and music critic, he was sometimes dubbed 'Irish Censor of Broadway' because of his relentless campaign against stage-Irishism. Show-business had its attractions; he selected dancing girls for the Ziegfeld Follies, was publicity manager for the booming Metro-Goldwyn Mayer film empire, for Victor Herbert, John McCormack and was on friendly terms with Sam Goldwyn, Mae West, Al Jolson, Jack Dempsey, Mick McTigue, John L. Sullivan and other celebrities.

Kruger acted also. A film mogul offered him a handsome contract, telling him that he was 'as sweet-looking a young divil as ever vamped a colleen bawn'.[1] His association with stars, starlets and hoofers made him a much sought-after friend. Theatre tycoons often called on him to supply willing dates and there is evidence that he himself enjoyed the company of glamorous young women. His influence in the business brought about a boycott of the stage-Irish film *Kathleen Mavourneen* until it was subjected to cuts. As he said himself: 'I took the fairies out of old men's ears, I took the ribbons off the pigs and the pigs out of the parlours. I shot down drunken Paddies trailing their coats on the road. I left the shamrocks and most of the Blarney but *Kathleen Mavourneen* hit the screen minus a lot of whiskey, a lot of shillelaghs and a lot of blood.'[2]

Kruger Kavanagh returned for good to his native Dunquin in June 1929. Seven years later he married Cáit Neill from Ballymore. Their guesthouse attracted intellectuals, writers, politicians, actors and artists, with whom the host spoke in Irish or English.

In his eighty-sixth year Kavanagh enjoyed a short return to the world of show-business when the David Lean film *Ryan's Daughter* was shot in and around Dunquin. Robert Mitchum, Sarah Miles, John Mills and Trevor Howard frequented the pub and listened to Kruger's stories – some true, others to be taken with the grain of salt that foreigners sometimes lacked. One concerned his taking his father's goat to a pucán [male goat] during his youth. The sea was so stormy that it lashed a huge wave up on the donkey-cart. Hearing the nanny screaming, Kruger looked around to discover a giant conger eel attempting to couple with her.

Kruger ran for election to the Kerry County Council on one occasion. He placed a notice in the local newspapers:

KERRY COUNTY COUNCIL
TRALEE AREA
DO GACH GAEL BOCHT AGUS NOCHT

I wish to announce to the voters of the above area and West Kerry
that I am going forward as an
INDEPENDENT CANDIDATE
To represent the People Only
No Party Blocks

Maurice (Kruger) Kavanagh, Dunquin.

All the aforesaid is as near to fact as can be discovered through the haze of colourful fiction surrounding Kruger.

Without mentioning the theme of this book, I asked a Dingleman about Kruger. He chuckled and said 'Lord, but he was a thundering rogue!' Then he hesitated and added 'a lovable rogue, of course' and went on to relate some of the yarns told around Dunquin and Dingle about its famed son.

'He came from a very clever family but being the eldest, he received the minimum of education so he became a conman instead. His brothers, Seán a' Cota (so called because of the long, cape-like coat he wore) and Seamus, the distinguished professor, were brilliant people. Kruger was a kind of a Walter Mitty, his features were like carved granite and he was popular with women – he was a bit of a Raymond Navarro. In the United States, he got a job as a janitor in a convent. When cleaning up one day he broke a statue of the Blessed Virgin or some saint. Knowing the trouble he would get into, he knelt down and wept until the nuns found him and were so touched by his 'piety' that they did not even chastise him.

'"The President of the United States sent for me once," Kruger would say. "I have a problem, Kruger. This world war is troublesome. Stalemate in the trenches and all that. So I invented an apparatus that could be thrown into the trenches, would explode and scatter the Germans." Kruger had heard about grenades, of course, and was trying to impress.

'When he came back to Kerry, he owned a naomhóg [currach-like boat]. A stipend was paid to him for delivering pensions, social welfare payments, dole and such things to the islanders. But sure it is sometimes said he kept collecting the payments for people who had died years before. If Kruger did not like somebody, he would throw a sheet around him and go out in the night and pretend he was a ghost or a banshee.'

'Then there was the classic court case before Judge

Johnson, who wrote *The Old Lady says No, The Moon on Yellow River* and other works. Kruger was seeking a licence for his pub, and was pleading the vast catchment area it would cover. He rattled off names, for instance, like Vicarstown, Báile an Bhiocáire, Uaigh an Spáinnigh, Doonmore, Gallán an tSagairt, Been Hill, Gable Hill and so on – but sure they were all names for the same places or townlands very close together.

'Established in the bar business, he stocked a beer called Patz because in so doing he became entitled to free glasses advertising the product. The cute Kerrymen were delighted because they realised very quickly that the Patz glass held a little more than the normal medium one. One day Kruger collected a consignment of the glasses, then called into Tom Long's in Dingle and called for a drink. Tom served it in the normal glass but Kruger protested and demanded a Patz glass. Tom poured the stout from one into the other and only then did Kruger realise how he was losing out in his bar. "Well fuck you Patz", he shouted, then dashed out to the car and smashed every glass in it.'

Paddy Kavanagh, Myles na Gopaleen, reprobates, actors, politicians, artists and writers frequented Kruger's. Upon the walls of the bar were hung photographs of the craggy-faced Kerryman posing with all sorts of celebrities – the Queen of Tonga, De Valera, Jack Dempsey, Mae West and God knows who else. Most of the pictures were inscribed 'To Kruger, from Jack' and so on. He could be very boastful and one night Brendan Behan got drunk and had a row with Kruger. When he was leaving the bar, Behan went over to a picture of the Sacred Heart and scrawled across it: 'To Kruger, from Jaysus'.

Ireland's most celebrated publican, adventurer and raconteur died on 15 April 1971.

10

WALKING GALLOWS

This wretch of whom we have but an imperfect account, was born in Upper Newcastle, Co. Wicklow c. 1766, bred an apothecary in Dublin ... Beneath [his] aspiring genius ... he united the character of a gentleman with those of judge and executioner.

Watty Cox's *The Irish Magazine* or the Monthly Asylum for Neglected Biography, January 1810.

There is more oral evidence than documentation on a despised militiaman who was a greatly feared rogue in Wicklow, Longford and elsewhere before and during the 1798 Rebellion. Indeed his conduct and that of others like him, helped to kindle the flames of that revolution. Edward Hepenstal was a lieutenant in the 88th Regiment and County Wicklow Militia. He was the third son of Edward Hepenstal of Newcastle. Over the years, other forms of spelling have been used, notably Hempenstall. The Derrycassin, Co. Longford family of Dopping-Hepenstal used the older spelling. In July 1858, Diana Dalrymple Hepenstal, grand-niece of Lieutenant Edward, married Ralph Anthony Dopping, to initiate that line.

The name, originally Dutch, is derived from a Yorkshire toponym and the family arrived in Wicklow in the early eighteenth century. They spread to Wexford and Dublin and in 1855 there were twenty-one families in the region. Edward, sometimes called Jack, was uncharacteristic of his rather gentle lineage and is best remembered by his nickname, Walking Gallows. He was so called because he was big and strong and often strangled victims in an unusual manner.

The normal method of hanging then was the traditional gallows – a rope slung from a cross-bar supported by two uprights. The process was drawn out, even to the extent that the victim was given copious drinks of water to refresh him between sequences. Hepenstal, however, simply placed a noose around rebels' necks and dragged them along the road after him while they screamed in pain until they died. The seven and a half foot high, handsome giant had two medium-sized assistants who strolled along at either side of him. They would catch young rebels and place the rope around their necks for their master to do his dirty work. The judge, historian, and Member of Parliament, Sir Jonah Barrington claimed to know Hepenstal well. He put his height at six feet and said:

> He could lift a ton, but could not leap a rivulet; he looked mild, and his address was civil – neither assuming nor at all ferocious from his countenance [I] should never have suspected him of cruelty; but so cold-blooded and so eccentric an executioner of the human race I believe never yet existed, save among the American Indians.
>
> His inducement to the strange barbarity he practised I can scarcely conceive; unless it proceeded from that natural taint of cruelty which so often distinguishes man above all other animals when his power becomes uncontrolled. The propensity was probably strengthened in him from the indemnities of martial law, and by those visions of promotion whereby violent partisans are perpetually urged, and so frequently disappointed.[1]

Leading up to and during the 1798 Rebellion, Hepenstal's judgment of rebels was arbitrary. If he disliked their appearance, he took action. Barrington ashamedly admits that this behaviour was the subject of jocularity among legal people:

What in other times he himself would have died for, as a murderer, was laughed at as the manifestation of loyalty: never yet was martial law so abused, or its enormities so hushed up. Being a military officer, the lieutenant conceived he had a right to do just what he thought proper, and to make the most of his time while martial law was flourishing.[2]

Walking Gallows had a bit of style about him. If there was not a rope handy, he used a drum rope or his own silk cravat which he claimed was softer on the victim's neck. He appears to have been called as extern hangman once to Kerry House, St Stephen's Green. Perhaps he felt that a job in the city demanded a little extra in the way of novelty so he introduced the 'trotting execution'. He wound his cravat into a rope, expertly slid it over a rebel's neck, and secured it by a double-knot. Hepenstal drew the cravat over his own shoulder while his assistant lifted the victim's heels. With a mighty chuck, the hangman drew the unfortunate's face over his shoulder, cheek-by-jowl with his own, then trotted around the cobbled yard imitating a bucking farm-horse 'the rebel choking and gulping meanwhile, until he had no further solicitude about sublunary affairs'.[3] A final chuck in case the neck was not already broken, and the corpse of another rebel was tossed on the ground for Hepenstal's aide to search for valuables. Walking Gallows operated in other areas besides Wicklow and Dublin. His regiment was stationed in Strabane for a period and he may have been dispatched southward from there. The regiment caused more than a stir when they advertised in the *Strabane Journal* of 20 April 1795:

Wanted for the service of the officers who compose the mess of His Majesty's Wicklow Regiment of Militia, twelve beautiful girls who have not inhabited the town of Strabane since the 5 of April ... As wages is by no means the object, it is expected that none will apply who do not produce a certificate signed by eight respectable matrons, of their having their virtue pure and unsullied. No girl will answer above the age of 18, or under that of 14. Application to be made to the regimental matron, Mrs Catherine Smyth, Bowling Green, Strabane. N.B. Growing girls of the age of 13 if approved and highly recommended may possibly be taken.

Hepenstal certainly operated in Longford and Westmeath and he seemed to carry out his evil practice en route from Wicklow because there is evidence of at least one hanging by him in Co. Kildare, at Carbury. He encountered a suspicious looking man there and without any evidence, decided he had to be a rebel plotting the death of the king and so disposed of him.

Pat Farrell of Ballinree was regarded as the biggest man in Longford. He was at least seven feet tall, had a barrel chest and was extremely muscular. After the battle of Ballinamuck, where the celebrated Gunner Magee held the axle of a field-piece in order to continue with its fire, Farrell retreated to Granard, whose topography offered excellent defensive features. Hepenstal, however, controlled Granard at the time and locals recorded that he 'jerked more men into eternity' than had been sent to their maker by violent death in the following four score years. In his *Historical Notes of County Longford* (1886), James P. Farrell states:

His method of hanging was novel in the extreme. Just let him catch a rebel – the rope was adjusted and slung across his shoulder, a pull and a sudden jerk, and the 'rebel's' days on earth were ended. People will wonder that such a wretch would be allowed to walk on green grass in the eighteenth century.

But back to Farrell in Granard. There was pandemonium there because General Lake was expected to turn up after his success at Ballinamuck and nearby Ballinalee, while Hepenstal was known to have gone to Cavan to summon troops from there. Farrell was given the task of defending the Finea entrance to Granard, where Hepenstal would arrive. When the two giants came face to face 'Farrell, with one ponderous blow of his broken sword-hilt, put Hepenstal *hors de combat*, and his ragged mob of yeomen soon after took to flight'.[4] About to pursue, Farrell was halted by news conveyed by a messenger. Lake was indeed leading a large contingent of the enemy and their arrival was imminent. With two colleagues, O'Keefe and Denison, Farrell organised the defence of Granard once more. Lake arrived and a vicious battle ensued.

Meanwhile, Hepenstal recovered and brought his Cavan troops back to the fight. Farrell's men were therefore being attacked on two fronts. Knowing the fate meted out to the rebels at Ballinamuck, Farrell realised there was no point in continuing the fight. He pivoted his men to the right and escaped down a narrow lane while Lake's and Hepenstal's men, still eagerly advancing, clashed and began fighting each other instead of the Longfordmen. Farrell, mounted on a white mare, lost Denison and his men. They were surrounded by Hepenstal and his Finea militia. Farrell discovered this and dashed to Denison's assistance. Hepenstal took note, took aim and fired. Farrell fell and the fight was over.

In recognition of splendid services rendered to the crown and to the constitution, Westmeath's grand jury voted a service of plate to the officers of the Wicklow militia at their midsummer assizes of 1797. In protest, a correspondent to *The Press*, a Dublin newspaper published only during 1797 and 1798, cited the conduct of Edward Hepenstal and berated the grand jury for using the money of ratepayers who were powerless to object to the presentation.

In north Westmeath at the time, a gang of bandits robbed and plundered where and when they could. On a stormy wet night in June they got drunk on poitín near Killare while awaiting the return of one of their men who was missing. They were worried, fearing he might inform the Athlone Yeomanry of their intention of robbing a coach. They went ahead with the hold-up and their doubts were proved genuine – its passengers, armed yeomen, fired on them. Three of the robbers were killed and the remainder were taken prisoner and brought to Mullingar. Two days later, the ringleader of the gang was brought to Moyvore and handed over to Lieutenant Hepenstal.

At a place then called Gardenstown, near Moyvore, Edward Carroll, a seventy-year-old blacksmith, lived with his three sons. All four were United Irishmen and they forged pikeheads for the anticipated rising. Information on their activities was passed on and Hepenstal was led to local cemeteries and bogs where the pikes were hidden. Then he arrived at the forge along with the informer and some militiamen. In the pleasant manner at which he was so adept, Walking Gallows explained all he knew but promised the old man and his sons protection if they handed over their merchandise quietly. Old Carroll complied but Hepenstal immediately killed him with a sabre. The sons were butchered too and their household, out-offices and haggard were set ablaze. The wife and child of one of the young Carrolls was in the kitchen at the time but one of the raiders rescued her. Hepenstal reluctantly let her go, calling her a bitch and warning her that if she ever returned or told of what happened, she too would be killed. Hepenstal threw the murdered bodies on a cart and proceeded to Moyvore village. There he arrested three other men, tied them to the shafts of the cart and travelled three miles to Ballymore. A Mrs Mc-

Cormick offered James Woods, author of *The Annals of Westmeath* a grotesque picture of the procession leaving a trail of blood as the dead men's entrails dropped down from the cart and became entangled and wound around its axle and wheelspokes. Beside the militia guarding the group, a drummer beat and a fifer played 'Croppies Lie Down'. Female relatives of the captured men wailed and screamed and those at the end of the group cursed Walking Gallows aloud. On reaching Ballymore, Hepenstal called on various landlords and invited them to witness some 'pigeon-shooting'. Some accepted but Lord Oxmanstown questioned Hepenstal's right to execute the men without a proper trial. With disdain, he told Oxmanstown that he was in charge. The arrested men pleaded that they were the sole support of widowed mothers, but they were manacled and forced to kneel down on the village green. Then Hepenstal ordered the militiamen to shoot.

Terrorised country folk would not assist the bereaved in wake and burial preparation; one neighbour offered a bed to carry the bodies to be buried in Moranstown. Forty houses in Moyvore were burned in the same incident and before leaving the district, Walking Gallows visited Ballymore fair. A farmer was holding out his hand to have it slapped in the age-old way of sealing a bargain for stock. Hepenstal almost severed the arm from the shoulder. A young mason begged for mercy on his knees; Hepenstal struck him down and left him dying. A priest went to give the last rites and three militiamen 'made a riddle of his body'.[5] Seventeen others were 'cut, maimed and abused [so] that many of them [were] rendered miserable objects for the remainder of their lives'.[6]

A great folk-history concerning Walking Gallows grew. His relatives disowned him; indeed it is not surprising that they denied kinship betimes. Historians argued the improbability of his deserving such notoriety. In particular, they doubted his hanging methods. On 8 August 1797, however, Hepenstal himself vouched for his *modus operandi*. At the trial of a William Kennedy, Edenderry, at Navan, the lieutenant told how he had tied a rope around the neck of the accused and threw him across his shoulder in order to extract information. Kennedy refused to talk and for once Walking Gallows submitted him for proper trial – presumably in the hope of eliciting more information. In the event, Kennedy still refused to inform and was executed. At another trial in Athy during September 1797, Hepenstal admitted to pricking a prisoner with a bayonet as well as using his familiar rope treatment.

When Lieutenant Edward Hepenstal died, his brother received a handsome pension from the government. Wicklow people like to claim that Walking Gallows was shot in Aughavanna and placed at the side of the road with a nettle planted in some mud that had been forced into his mouth. His corpse was left to decompose and receive the ridicule of passers-by.[7] Soldiers came and attempted to bury Walking Gallows on the land of a farmer named O'Toole, but he refused permission. Others followed his example. Eventually he was buried opposite a public house at Raheen. Markers were placed at the head and foot of the grave to show the size of the executioner and hundreds visited the grave to express derision.

Watty Cox's *The Irish Magazine* (January 1810) disagrees and says Hepenstal died in his bed at his brother's house in St Andrew's Street in 1804. He had developed 'the most shocking distemper [and] his body was literally devoured by vermin'. Francis Higgins, the Sham Squire (*q.v.*), recorded in his journal of 18 September 1800:

Died on Thursday night, of a dropsical complaint, Lieutenant Edward Hepenstall [sic], of the 68th Regiment [sic], sometime back an officer in the Wicklow militia – a gentleman whose intrepidity and spirit during the Rebellion rendered much general good, and himself highly obnoxious to traitors.

Higgins followed with a tribute to 'the qualities which endeared Mr Hepenstal to his family and friends' and gives St Andrew's churchyard as Hepenstal's burial place.[8]

Sir Jonah Barrington's wry comment was:

Providence, however, which is said to do 'every thing for the best', (though some persons who are half starving, and others who think themselves very unfortunate, will not allow it so much credit) determined that Lieutenant H_____'s loyalty and merits should meet their full reward in another sphere – where, being quite out of reach of all his enemies, he might enjoy his destiny without envy or interruption. It therefore, very soon after the rebellion had terminated, took the lieutenant into its own especial keeping; and dispatched a raging fever to bring him off to the other world, which commission the said fever duly executed after twenty-one day's combustion; – and no doubt his ghost is treated according to its deserts; but nobody having since returned from those regions to inform us what has actually become of the lieutenant, it is still a dead secret, and I fancy very few persons in Ireland have any wish for the opportunity of satisfying their curiosity. People however give a shrewd guess, that it is possible he may be employed somewhere else in the very same way wherein he entertained himself in Ireland; and that after being duly furnished with a tail, horns, and cloven foot, no spirit could do infernal business better than the lieutenant.[9]

It was also suggested at one time that the uninscribed grave of Walking Gallows should bear the epitaph:

Here lie the bones of Hepenstal
Judge, jury, gallows, rope and all.

The infamous gentleman's widow married a celebrated Dr Patrick Duignan. Sixty years after his death, Hepenstal's nearest living relative wrote to *The Irish Times* debunking all that had been written about Walking Gallows as fable. Because Sir Jonah Barrington and others had used a mere initial 'Lieutenant H____', it was argued there was no evidence of its referring to Edward Hepenstal. Furthermore, wrote the correspondent,

> The acts ... were not committed by Lieut H, whose character was in the first instance traduced for party purposes, and blackened by the exaggeration and additions of the dupes to whom the story was told. He was as wholly incapable of such conduct as his appearance and manners seemed to indicate, and the instances given of his cruelty are as little founded in fact as the popular story (accounting for the time and place of his burial being not generally known) that he had been carried off by a familiar which had attended him during life in the shape of a 'black cow'.[10]

William J. Fitzpatrick's account in 'The Informers of '98' was disputed so that author replied to *The Irish Times* reiterating his views and quoting other reliable sources in which Hepenstal's full name had been used. 'The face is not always an index to the mind' he said, in answer to the claim that Hepenstal had benign features and continued:

> Before the sweeping denial can be accepted that Hepenstal's exploits gave him, by general consent, the nickname of 'walking gallows', it is necessary, not only to erase historic record, but to attempt to silence the irrepressible voice of song. A ballad of the day, professing to come from some ultra-loyalist, concludes:

> > 'Now what evil can befall us,
> > Since we have got our walking gallows'.[11]

11

'FULL OF RASCALITY'

Tim Quillinan

On the bank of the Togher river near Oola, Co. Limerick, stands Castletown Castle, known locally as Quillinan Castle. Tom Quillinan was involved in the great mass-movement of 1879–82 known as the 'land war'. Evictions in his home county and nearby Tipperary angered him and he decided to teach the English troops a lesson. He had information delivered to them that a strong force of Land Leaguers had occupied Castletown Castle. At the same time he spread news for miles around that large scale evictions were about to take place in Oola.

Hundreds gathered on the Oola hills on a May day and watched the Coldstream Guards arrive in full battle array and put in their assault on the castle. The edifice looked formidable to strangers but the gathered assembly knew it was an empty ruin harbouring nothing more dangerous than a few jackdaws. They laughed with derision when the red-faced military discovered their mistake.

Somehow, the affair was reported on an Italian newspaper and Archbishop Croke received a letter from the Vatican expressing the Pope's apprehension about his lack of control over his rebellious flock.

Thomas Cuffe

A public house in Kilbeggan, Co. Westmeath was said to have got its name, 'The Volunteer', because a member of the eighteenth century Irish Volunteers died on the premises. It was here that the dastardly viceroy, Lord Townsend, rested one evening and became excessively drunk. The innkeeper, Thomas Cuffe, plied him with liquor and did not demur when the viceroy drew his sword and ordered him to kneel. Cuffe did so and Townsend there and then touched his shoulder with the sword-blade and murmured words bestowing knighthood.

Next morning, the viceroy thanked the landlord for his excellent table, room and drink but Cuffe reminded him of what he had done in his cups. Townsend shrugged the incident off as a joke but Cuffe insisted that he was now a Lord. Then Townsend tried bribery and offered twenty guineas for silence on the matter. Again Cuffe refused, cannily saying: 'For myself, your viceroyship, it matters nothing but her Ladyship wouldn't hear of it, so she wouldn't!'

Buck Whaley

In his memoirs, the celebrated eighteenth century Dublin buck, Thomas Whaley boasted of spending his considerable inheritance before he was thirty-four. Gambling and other extravagances led to his ruination but he enjoyed every minute of his hectic life.

In one evening's card-playing, he once lost £14,000. For a Grand Tour, he was allotted £900 per annum for incidental expenses, a sum that proved totally inadequate.

Whaley fitted well into the category 'likable rogue',

the 'hard man' beloved of his metropolitan contemporaries. Dining once with the Duke of Leinster, he was asked where he intended travelling next. Without thinking he replied, 'Jerusalem'. At the time, such a journey was hazardous; bandits roamed the Middle East and the Ottoman Empire, in the last stages of decline, was less than accommodating to pilgrims. So his fellow bucks bet Whaley £15,000 that he could not make the trip. If he did not return within two years with proof of his being in the Holy City, he would forfeit the money. He left Dublin in July 1788.

> *One morning walking George's Quay,*
> *A monstrous crowd stopped up the way;*
> *They came to see a sight so rare*
> *A sight that made old Dublin stare.*

Past the Kent coast he sailed with his galleys stocked with Madeira and a complement of servant-sailors. The Gibraltar garrison held a ball in Buck's honour. Dressed as Turks, he and his retinue moved to Constantinople where Whaley was so impressive that he received a permit to visit Jerusalem. He reached his destination and received a certificate from the mother superior of Nazareth Convent stating that he resided there two nights.

Having returned and collected his winnings he gambled at Daly's Club, kept a mistress by whom he had children and on one occasion threw himself out of a window on to a cab that bore a lady to whom he was attracted. He missed and was seriously injured.

It was while engaged in politics that Whaley displayed genuine roguery. At a young age he held the Newcastle, Co. Down seat but later, sitting in Enniscorthy, he accepted a £4,000 bribe to support the Union; a more substantial offer persuaded him to oppose it!

His final years were disastrous. Forced to sell all his property to pay his debts, married and trying to educate children, he fled to the Isle of Man. To win yet another bet that he could live on Irish soil without inhabiting Ireland, he imported earth for the foundations of his new home.

Buck Whaley died at a Cheshire inn in 1800, aged thirty-four. After his coffin was closed, an Irishman named Robinson danced a jig on it.

Martin Thornton

In the 1940s, as always, Professional Irish Heavyweight Boxing was a hit and miss affair with people like Ernie Simmonds of Dublin winning the crown from Dom Lydon of Mayo but never defending it. Chris Cole of Mullingar beat a giant of a man, Jim Cully of Tipperary but on his first defence of the title, lost it to Pat Mulcahy of Dublin and Cork. He failed in turn to retain it when Paddy O'Sullivan of Mourne Abbey, Cork, a former Golden Gloves champion, beat him. Then came Martin Thornton of Cois Fairrge, Spiddal, Co Galway.

Dublin bookmaker Joe Mirrelson promoted the fight which took place in the Theatre Royal on 4 February 1944 in aid of the Lord Mayor's Coal Fund. Pat O'Connor and Pat Mulcahy featured in another title fight and on the bill also were Jimmy Ingle, fighting Spike McCormack for a £100 purse, winner take all. O'Sullivan had been fighting professionally for seven years and the people of Galway were on edge for the encounter. Martin's earlier fights were won in knockouts against people like Al Hayes, 'Cast Iron' Casey, Ben Valentine, Tom Reddington and others. By the time he met Sullivan he was known as the 'Connemara Crusher'.

Martin's mother was proud and excited but would

not travel to Dublin to see her son fight. In Galway, there were rumours of his being seen there the week before the fight when he should have been training, but it was later alleged that he was in a Dublin hospital receiving treatment for a back ailment.

People walked miles to houses that had wireless sets and went wild when, after eight minutes and fifty-six seconds, Thornton knocked his opponent into insensibility. A special report in the *Connaught Tribune* said:

> A fighting fury packed more dynamic action than was provided in the other 3½ hours of the night's fighting. [Thornton's] non-stop attack sent O'Sullivan reeling from pillar to post and brought the 4,000 spectators to their feet in a frenzy of excitement that has never before been equalled in the history of Irish boxing.

The frenzy was equalled back in Spiddal when Thornton took the microphone and spoke from the ring in his native tongue:

> Tá athás orm go bhfuair mé an buaidh anocht agus tá súil agam go mbeid mé ag troid annso arís go maith.

Thornton made a triumphant return to Galway, where he was met at the railway station by the Mayor and members of the Corporation. He promised to defend his newly-won title in Galway for its Mayor's charity fund. Jack London would be his prey after that, Martin vowed.

On 8 March Thornton knocked out Al Robinson in the third round. A notice in the *Connaught Tribune*, 11 March called a public meeting to organise a presentation to Martin. The Galway Chamber of Commerce wanted to promote the next fight. £54. 12s. was collected and when it was presented, Martin promised to retire from the ring in two years to look after a business premises he had just purchased in Spiddal. Before that, however, he hoped to beat Freddie Mills for the British and empire title.

Meanwhile, Martin found time to marry May Fahy of Tuam and the couple spent their honeymoon in Dublin. Seamus Kelly, Quidnunc in the *Irish Times*, told of a visit from Martin to his office:

> A huge youth came in here yesterday with a broken nose, jet black hair, yellow shoes and shoulders like a pair of grand pianos.

He boasted about meeting Mills and how easy it would be to beat him. Max Schmeling was in his sights too – and even world champion, Joe Louis. Weren't they saying so in the Connemara notes of the *Tribune?* Thornton looked for the file of 5 February and all stories and features about himself. All the while he was shadow boxing around Kelly's head. Seamus wrote in his column:

> He wants copies of all our editions carrying stories about himself. The ghastly thing is that all those particular back-numbers are sold out. See you in the accident ward!

This was the period known as 'The Emergency', when a world war gave neutral Ireland the chance to develop its own professional boxing culture. The attraction of foreign travel was denied to amateurs and people like Jimmy Ingle could earn as much for one fight as they would working hard for a week at a timber mill. Gerry Egan was the main promoter of the period, and he had a keen publicist's angle on his fights. For example, he presented Ireland's tallest man, Jim Cully from Tipperary as 'Ireland's Carnera'. Professional boxing was renowned for its roguishness and Martin Thornton was a controversial member of the gallery of that ilk. But he was on top of the world in February 1945 when he again beat O'Sullivan, this time by a knockout in the first round.

As reigning Irish champion, Thornton drew the attention of English promoter, Jack Solomons who matched him against England's and the empire's champion, popular glamour-boy, Bruce Woodcock, a man who had previously beaten Martin soundly in Manchester. The fight took place on 24 August 1945. Some journalists believed, like Martin himself, that this would lead to a crack at the world heavyweight title held by Joe Louis. The venue was again the Theatre Royal in Dublin. Supporting bouts included John Ingle *v* Jimmy Smith in an Irish Lightweight Title Fight, Spike McCormack *v* Paddy Lyons, the north of England middleweight champion and Jimmy Ingle *v* Tommy Davis, a Welsh middleweight. Ingle was also a sparring partner for Thornton at Mount Street Club before the fight. Ireland was on its toes. The Theatre Royal was sold out and wireless batteries were being charged across the land. I had an autographed photograph of Thornton, shamrock on trunks, drop on nose, on my bedroom wall and was as despondent as any of the thousands of fans after the event. Press reports told how Thornton was nervous before the fight, in marked contrast to Woodcock's coolness and pristine condition. Thornton's normal dynamic start, as against O'Sullivan and others, was expected but on this occasion he approached his opponent with his chin tucked into his collar-bone. Obviously, he was intent on avoiding undue punishment rather than adopting an attacking spirit. Bruce Woodcock spotted Thornton's only exposed spot and pummelled his left eye. Through two rounds, Martin maintained his uninspired performance and already Dublin's wits were beginning to hum the 'Blue Danube', their traditional jibe of disapproval for tardy fighters. In round three, Thornton stuck out his tongue at Woodcock. The audience roared disapproval and called upon him to fight. Moving to his corner at the end of the round, Thornton asked Andy Smyth, the Belfast referee, to stop the fight. He refused and seconds later, a towel fluttered from one of Martin's seconds. One reporter spoke of Woodcock's smart appearance and added 'The only thing clean about Thornton was the towel flung from his corner.'

As Thornton slunk to his dressing-room amid jeers and bottle-throwing, there was an unprecedented scene in the auditorium as his fight-fans applauded the Englishman Bruce Woodcock.

Next day the papers asked questions. The *Evening Herald* wanted to know where was the dynamic energy, the Irish blood, the killer spirit that had demolished Pat O'Sullivan and Butcher Howell. Then it transpired that the wily Connemaraman had insisted on being paid his £800 fee before the fight. Some said he blackmailed Solomons by refusing, at the last minute, to go into the ring until the money was handed over. Thornton himself would later boast, to customers in An Draighneán Donn [The Blackthorn Bush] pub in Spiddal, that he threw the fight for a sum of £4,000 and added another £10,000 to his winnings by betting on Woodcock. Three weeks after the fiasco, the Irish Boxing Board of Control met to discuss the issue.

The Board used to meet in a room over Terry Rogers' turf accountant's office in Talbot Street. They found themselves in a dilemma because Thornton's purse had already been paid, so they could not demand a forfeiture. Instead, they revoked his Irish heavyweight title and suspended him *sine die*. Unfit and ageing, Martin made a brief re-appearance in the ring four years later at Belfast's Ulster Hall. The fight was stopped after three rounds against Ray Wilding. So ended Thornton's boxing career, not unimpressive with twenty-five wins out of thirty-six fights, all but two within the distance.

In his retirement, Martin became a bit like Kruger Kavanagh in Dingle – telling stories 'to beat the band' about his escapades within and outside the ring. He got his come-uppance from the Irish writer, Máirtín Ó Cadhain who was then a recruiting officer for the IRA. Speaking in Irish, the two Máirtíns were criticising the British occupation of the six counties and Thornton remarked that every one of the British should be beaten out of the country. Ó Cadhain replied wryly: 'You had only one to beat and you made a damn bad job of it!' Still Thornton boasted and as late as 1981 he told a *Sunday Press* journalist that he had been paid £4,000 to take a dive against Woodcock.

> While alive, Thornton himself, every once in a while, provided a gullible journalist with a new 'true version' of what happened that night. Rarely in the history of professional boxing can so insignificant a fight have remained for so long of public interest.[1]

Thornton made a considerable amount of money dealing in cattle. He played handball and was a celebrated poacher. In the fisheries of the west of Ireland this gave a man significant status for few natives approved of their waters being preserved for the gentry.

A story is told in Spiddal of how a vigilant policeman made many attempts to catch Martin in the act so that he could prosecute, but the poacher always eluded him. One evening he came upon Thornton as he was leaving a preserved river with a fine salmon in his hand. Quick as a wink, the poaching boxer ran under a low bridge. The policeman knew that if he pursued Martin through one opening, he would easily escape through the other. So he waited, hoping for assistance to arrive or for Thornton to surrender with cold feet! Neither occurred, but after dusk Thornton made a sudden dash from the bridge, upended the policeman by striking him a mighty blow with the fish and made his escape.

The police raided An Draighneán Donn often too, for the Thornton establishment kept very late hours. Martin had a habit of running upstairs and calling down to his customers if he saw the police. One night, they had all escaped through the back door except a very lame old gardener who was too slow to move. Thornton tried to shove him through a side-window but the poor man got stuck in it and was abandoned there by Martin who returned and spent some time placating the gardaí. The police surrounded the pub another night so escape through the back yard was impossible. Thornton saw this when he checked from the top windows, so he rushed out the back door, whipped up a handful of stones and pelted them at the gardaí until they retreated.

He was prosecuted and brought to court. A sergeant gave evidence, saying that Thornton was flinging the stones and that they were hopping all around his men in the yard. Thornton denied this and the Justice asked him could he prove that he was not throwing stones at the gardaí. Thornton replied: 'If I was flinging stones at those fellows, you can be sure I wouldn't have missed them'. The District Justice could do little but laugh.

A more unsavoury side to Thornton's life is alleged by some of his contemporaries. A boastful womaniser, his escapades included having affairs with a mother and her daughter at the same time, they claim. One went as far as saying that he was a bigamist but this was vehemently denied by those who knew him better. Cases of intimidating buyers and sellers at fairs with threats are cited by a man who says 'Máirtín' became the most unpopular man in Spiddal. 'He had notions about himself at football too'. A member of Galway Fire Brigade had a reputation of being accomplished at arm-wrestling – the accepted pub method of judging superior strength. A bet of £100 was laid for a match between this exponent and Thornton but Thornton, afraid of losing, kept offering excuses and eventually backed out of the contest completely. For some time, Martin was a 'bouncer' in the elegant new Teach Furbo [Furbo House, a hotel], in a small seaside resort near his native village. He was in great demand by visiting Americans who revelled in his tales of past glory. While working at the dying craft of thatching near his native Spiddal on 1 October 1982, Martin Thornton, rogue-boxer suffered a massive heart attack and died. He was sixty-eight years of age.

Why Jinks?

A fool or a rogue? The man who cannot be figured out is often given the benefit of the doubt and instead of being dubbed 'a cute hoor' is called a questionable rogue. The spirit of one man may contest his inclusion, but Alderman John Jinks of Sligo certainly has left political commentators puzzled since 1927.

On 11 August of that year, Eamon de Valara and his Fianna Fáil deputies took their seats in the Dáil for the first time, De Valera insisting that he had brushed the bible aside, signed a book and therefore had not taken the oath of allegiance to the crown. Alderman Jinks was a member of the National League Party founded in 1926 by Captain William Redmond, John Redmond's son. Advocating co-operation with Britain and Northern Ireland, they won eight seats in the June election of 1927. In an attempt to oust W.T. Cosgrave's Cumann na nGaedheal government, Redmond agreed to support Fianna Fáil and Labour when on 16 August 1927, Thomas Johnson, Labour party leader, brought about a vital division by proposing that the Executive Council had ceased to retain majority support in the Dáil. During the debate, deputy Vincent Rice of the National League rejected the alliance and supported the Executive Council and Jinks was not in the chamber for the vote. There were seventy-one for and against and the Ceann Comhairle's casting vote decided in favour of the Executive Council.

All sorts of reasons were ventured for the absence of John Jinks. The most popular explanation was that Jinks was lunched on that day by two Cosgrave supporters: the celebrated editor of *The Irish Times*, R.M. Smyllie and Major Bryan Cooper, an Independent deputy. They lavished hospitality on their fellow townsman and Jinks was put to bed in the hotel (or on the Sligo train) while Cooper returned to the Dáil to vote.

Some observers claim that Jinks listened to the debate and decided to abstain, simply by disappearing. They say he calmly returned to the chamber next day, wondering what all the fuss was about.

> Seán Lemass declared that henceforward the Cosgrave government held office only 'by the good will of a gentleman from Sligo whose name is – or who did not answer to the name of – John Jinks' but the grass-roots never forgot. At the next general election, the most famous TD of the time was defeated.[2]

Whatever the reason for his absence, John Jinks said nothing. The Dáil was dissolved on 27 August. The National Stud bought a racehorse the following year and Cosgrave suggested the name 'Mr Jinks'. The horse won the English 2000 Guineas in 1929!

Notes

Chapter 1

1. *Freeman's Journal*, 21 October 1766.
2. No. 1782.
3. State Paper Office, Frazer Manuscripts.
4. William J. Fitzpatrick, *The Sham Squire* (Dublin 1865).
5. *Ibid*.
6. William J. Fitzpatrick, *Ireland before the Union* (Dublin 1880).
7. Watty Cox's *The Irish Magazine*, October 1810. F.W. Conway became editor of the *Freeman's Journal* after Higgins's death.

Chapter 2

1. June Rose, *The Perfect Gentleman* (London 1977).
2. Bulmley To Barry, 14 January 1805, National Library of Ireland.
3. It is a sweet and seemly thing to die for one's country.
4. William L. Pressly, 'Portrait of a Cork Family: The Two James Barrys', *Cork Historical and Archaeological Society Journal* Vol. XC No. 249 January–December 1985. Note 57. Margaret Bulkley to John Bulkley, Barry Family Albums.
5. *Ibid*. Note 63. James Barry to General de Miranda, *Archivo del General Miranda*.
6. Isabel Rea, *The Strange Story of Dr James Barry* (London 1958).
7. *Manchester Guardian*, 21 August 1865.

(A play, *Colours – Jane Barry Esq.* by Jean Binnie was premiered at the Abbey Theatre, Dublin on 3 October 1988 as part of the Dublin Millennium Theatre Festival. Ms Binnie's assistance in the compilation of the foregoing is acknowledged.)

Chapter 3

1. Magrath to Privy Council 12 October 1582. L. Ó Mearáin, *Clogher Record*, Vol 2 No.1. (1957).
2. Somerset R. L. Belmore, 'The Castle and Territory of Termon Magrath', *Ulster Journal of Archaeology* Vol IX No. 3 (1903).
3. *Ibid*.
4. F.J. Bigger, *UJOA* Vol XII (1906).
5. *Ibid*.

6. Rev. J. Graves, *Royal Society of Antiquities Journal*, Vol II (1958).
7. *UJOA* Vol IX No. 3 (1903).
8. *Ibid*.
9. *Ibid*.

Chapter 4

1. Election literature, 1932 Election,NLI LO p.117, Item 105.
2. Alfie Byrne's scrap book, NLI LO, 2336.
3. *The Irish Times*, 28 – 30 December 1932.
4. Kathleen Clarke, *Revolutionary Woman* (Dublin 1991).

Chapter 5

1. Peter Fleming, *Invasion 1940* (London 1957).
2. Winston Churchill, *War Speeches Vol 1*, Ed. Charles Eade (London 1951).
3. J.A. Cole, *Lord Haw Haw* (London 1964).
4. Copy of letter in possession of Wm Naughton.

Chapter 6

1. John Edward Walsh, *Ireland Sixty Years Ago* (Dublin 1847).
2. Sir Jonah Barrington, *Personal Sketches of his own Times*, 3 Vols (London, 1830–2).

Chapter 7

(The author wishes to acknowledge details of Jack Doyle's love life and other information gleaned from Michael Taub's book *Jack Doyle – Fighting for Love* (London 1990), *The Fighting Irish* by Patrick Myler (Dingle 1987), *Ringside Seat*, by Peter Wilson (London 1948), and the *Evening Herald*, 5 May 1990.

Chapter 8

1. Barnaby Rich, 'New Description of Ireland', quoted by Edward MacLysaght, *Irish Life in the Seventeenth Century* (Cork 1950).
2. John Dunton's Letters, Bodleian Library, Oxford.
3. Mary E. Daly, *Dublin – the Deposed Capital* (Cork 1984).
4. Oliver St John Gogarty, *Tumbling in the Hay* (London 1939).
5. James Joyce, *Ulysses* (London 1936).
6. *Ibid*.
7. Seamus de Burca, *The Soldier's Song* (Dublin 1957).

8. Brendan Behan, *The Quare Fellow*, Act One, (London 1956).
9. Seamus de Burca, *The End of Mrs Oblong* (Dublin 1975).

Chapter 9

1. Seán Ó Lúíng, *Kruger* (1986).
2. *Ibid*.

Chapter 10

1. Sir Jonah Barrington, *Personal Sketches of his Own Times*, 3 Vols (London 1830–2).
2. *Ibid*.
3. *Ibid*.
4. James P. Farrell, *Historical Notes of County Longford* (Longford 1886).
5. James Woods, *Annals of Westmeath* (Dublin 1907).
6. *Ibid*.
7. *Beáloideas* (The Journal of the Folklore of Ireland Society), Nollaig 1935.
8. William J. Fitzpatrick, *The Sham Squire* (Dublin 1866). Some sources claim Rathfarnham as the burial place. From 1710, Hepenstals had been entombed there. Watty Cox gives Hepenstal's brother's house in St Andrew's Street as the place of death, adding 1804 as the year and the melodramatic description: '*the agonies of his suffering were aggravated by the most awful expressions, declaring the tortures of a soul apparantly surrounded with all the impatient messengers of hell from whose embraces he attempted to escape, until the most excruciating torments exhausted the struggling materials of mortality.*'
9. Barrington, *op. cit.*
10. Wm. J. Fitzpatrick, *Ireland before the Union* (Dublin 1880).
11. *Ibid*.

Chapter 11

1. Patrick Myler, *The Jimmy Ingle Story* , Dingle 1984.
2. John Cowell, *Sligo* (Dublin 1989).

SUPERSTITIONS OF IRISH COUNTRY PEOPLE

Padraic O'Farrell

Do you know why it is considered unlucky to meet a barefooted man, to start a journey on the tenth of November, to get married on a Saturday?

Irish country people believe that angels are always present among them and that all good things – crops, rain and so forth come from them. Bad spirits bring sickness to humans, animals and pestilence to crops. They do not speak of fairies on Wednesdays and Fridays for on those days *they* could be present while still being invisible.

Living in its fullest sense is still dear to the Irish country folk and is reflected in their customs. In the countryside life still has dignity and people are not mere statistics. Going to work, to sea, to weddings, wakes – at all of these there are fascinating customs to be observed.

GEMS OF IRISH WISDOM:
IRISH PROVERBS AND SAYINGS

Padraic O'Farrell

Gems of Irish Wisdom is a fascinating collection of Irish proverbs and sayings.

The tallest flowers hide the strongest nettles.
The man who asks what good is money has already paid for his plot.
A man begins cutting his wisdom teeth the first time he bites off more than he can chew.
Even if you are on the right track, you'll be run over if you stay there.
The road to heaven is well signposted but badly lit at night.
Love is like stirabout, it must be made fresh every day.
The begrudger is as important a part of Irish life as the muck he throws.
Love at first sight often happens in the twilight.
The man who hugs the altar-rails doesn't always hug his own wife.
If a man fools me once, shame on him. If he fools me twice, shame on me.
God never closes one door but He opens another.
Hating a man doesn't hurt him half as much as ignoring him.
Every cock crows on his own dunghill.
A kind word never gets a man into trouble.

HOW THE IRISH SPEAK ENGLISH

Padraic O'Farrell

How the Irish Speak English is a colourful and fascinating collection of the sayings and expressions which are still used by the Irish today. Padraic O'Farrell presents them unleavened with folklore and local history and if they are sometimes extended into 'yarns' who will quibble? – for Irish wit and humour at their best are contained in everyday anecdotes.

Talk away – your tongue is no scandal
That fellow would skin a flea for a ha'penny
I was pushing an open door
She had too much mileage up
Run your lamps over that
You won't tear in the plucking
I'll give you Paddy Ryan's supper
You'd see more flesh on a tinker's stick after a row
I'll give you £5 and the run of your teeth

Little-known words such as 'schraums', 'kelters', 'grawls', 'gommerils' are explained within suitable contexts and the examples quoted help to illuminate the byways of 'Irish' English.

IRISH FAIRY TALES

Michael Scott

'He found he was staring directly at a leprechaun. The small man was sitting on a little
mound of earth beneath the shade of a weeping
willow tree ... The young man could feel his
heart beginning to pound. He had seen lepre-
chauns a few times before but only from a distance. They were very hard to catch, but if you
managed at all to get hold of one ...'

Michael Scott's exciting stories capture all the
magic and mystery of Irish folklore. This collection of twelve fairy tales, beautifully and unus-
ually illustrated, include:

A HISTORY OF IRISH FAIRIES

Carolyn White

Whether you believe in fairies or not you cannot ignore them and here for the first time is *A History of Irish Fairies*. Having no stories directly from the fairies themselves, we must rely on descriptions by mortal men and women. A large part of this book is concerned with the relations between mortals and fairies, so that the reader may determine the best way to behave whenever he encounters fairies. The book contains such interesting details as the distinction and confusion between cluricaun and leprechaun and the fact that only male infants are stolen from the cradle. You can read about the Far Darrig, Merrows and Silkies, Banshees and Keening, the Lianhan Shee, Pookas, Dullahans and Ghosts.

In *A History of Irish Fairies* we find all the magic of the 'wee people'. The author deals with their important place in country folklore and tells us of their mannerisms, clothing, food and love-life.

THE MIDNIGHT COURT:
A DUAL LANGUAGE BOOK

A new translation by Patrick C Power

This is a racy, word-rich, bawdy poem; full of uncompromising language and attributes which have earned it increasing admiration and popularity since it was first composed by Brian Merriman in 1780. The bachelor uninterested in marriage and the aged bone-cold married man, the spouse-hunting lady and the dissatisfied spinster; the celebration of a woman's right to sex and marriage; disapproval of clerical celibacy – all these elements form part of the subject-matter of *The Midnight Court*.

Years ago, few speakers of Irish were without some knowledge of this full-blooded piece of literature, while very many people could recite the entire thousand and more lines of *The Midnight Court* in the version popular in their own area. It is one of the most interesting as well as the most entertaining survivals of the literature of Gaelic Ireland in the Penal times when humour, irony, literary tradition and sense of proportion had not fallen victims to oppression and humiliation.

The translation supplied with this edition of Merriman's poem is an endeavour to come as near as possible to the rural expression and attitudes which are part and parcel of the style of the original. Although actual use of the dialect is avoided, the translator has used words and modes of expression occasionally which are found in English as spoken in the Irish countryside.